STUMP.

A Campaign Journal

STUMP.
A Campaign Journal

by Stump Connolly

DEAD TREE PRESS
CHICAGO

Designed by R Jamie Apel
Character Concept: Casey Stockdon
Executive Editor: Scott Jacobs
Associate Executive Editor: Bruce Bendinger
Assistant Associate Executive Editor: Melissa Davis
Assistant Assistant Associate Executive Editor: Kevin Heubusch
Publisher: Lorelei Davis Bendinger

Library of Congress Cataloging-in-Publication Data
Connolly, Stump
STUMP A Campaign Journal

Includes index
ISBN 1-887229-03-5

First Printing August, 1997

To Ben and Justin

//stump.stuff
@ contents

Introduction

A new scam... A dying breed... somebody has to be there when they spill the gravy.

The telephone rang. It was Hillman, our man on the campaign trail, covering, as we say, the presidential race for the *Dallas Morning News*. "When you coming out?" he screeched.

"I'm not," I said. "I've got a new scam. I'm going to cover it all on the internet. Read the papers. Watch TV. And if I miss anything, I'll download the Quicktime Clip."

"Aw, Stump," Hillman said. "When are you going to give up on this new-fangled technology? Won't you miss the road?"

"Miss all those Waffle Houses in Texas? Miss the train rides through Georgia and chicken and pea luncheons in Dayton? Miss New Hampshire in February? Miss the Green Daisy Inn in Charlotte in March? Miss the Secret Service, the luggage checks, the bomb detectors, the damned dogs?" I said. "No way, no how. The farthest I intend to travel this year is from the TV to the refrigerator, and I'll stop in at my computer every once in a while to see if I have any e-mail."

"Well, it's just as well. It ain't the same out here," Hillman said. "There are no more boys on the bus. Hunter, Stout, Leubsdorf. They're all gone. There ain't no bus anymore. It's all zone coverage. We got one in the air and one in the field, issue desks back at the home shop, regional coverage, co-ordinating producers. We even got a guy who just watches TV -- and gets paid for it!"

"It's a sad world, Hillman," I said. "You're a dying breed."

"Oh, there's still a few of us left," he said. "Someone's got to be there when they spill the gravy on their suit."

"I'll tell you what. If anything happens out there, you give me a call. You want to see what's happening in the real world, you can just dial up my homepage," I said.

"Your what?" Hillman said.

"My homepage. It's where I publish my opinions every week. People call it up and they read them," I said. "It's like journalism without newspapers."

"They read 'em! Well then, who needs me?" he said.

"Somebody has to be there when they spill the gravy," I said. **"See you on the tarmac."**

Iowa Feeding Frenzy

I have a recurring nightmare.

I am standing in the polling place waiting to vote and all the media in the world comes up to ask me who I'm voting for and why. Before I even get out, they've broadcast my opinion, elected the man, and he's taking the oath of office. I walk out and say, "I changed my mind." But it's too late. That nightmare is Iowa.

I used to think the way Iowa conducted caucuses instead of primaries was kind of quaint. In the case of George McGovern in 1972, it was even useful: giving ordinary citizens a way of venting their frustration over how the war in Vietnam was going.

But times, alas, have changed. And so have politics.

The Iowa caucuses are not a forum for political discussion, but a launching pad for political campaigns. Stephen Forbes, for instance, reportedly spent $4 million on TV ads in Iowa and bought himself 9,000 votes -- at about $450 per vote. Lamar Alexander -- who's he, you said yesterday. Oh, Lamar Alexander, sure I know him, he finished third -- spent 80 days in the state and got 17,000 people to vote for him. Bob Dole -- the guy we all know is going to win the Republican nomination eventually -- won the goddam primary with 26,000 votes and got trashed for it in the media.

What's going on here? It's a feeding frenzy for the political junkies in the media who've been sitting around Washington all winter fighting off cabin fever.

Let's put this thing in perspective. The number of people who turned out this February to make Bob Dole a winner in Iowa was fewer than the number of people who turn out for a day game in April at Wrigley field.

And yet, the ABC, NBC, and CBS news teams don't exactly descend on Wrigley Field every April to take the pulse of the nation. But they descended on Iowa this year -- and they brought with them all the anchors and anchorettes for *The Morning News, Today, Good Morning America, Nightline, CNN Tonight* and pretty much every other TV personality who ever lapped at the trough of political power.

And believe you me, it's not because Iowa is important.

There are only 1 million eligible voters in Iowa. Less than 10 percent go to the Republican caucuses. They elect 2,100 of their peers to go to a state convention where about 25 fellow Republicans are selected to attend the Republican National Convention in San Diego in August. There -- amid the excitement of a Republican convention (is that an oxymoron?) -- they are the 28th most important state delegation.

If the networks were embarrassed to be there -- and who could watch them without sensing it -- imagine how embarrassing it was to be a candidate. You travel around in the middle of winter to a bunch of small towns --

generically known as Des Moines -- and answer really important questions like what's your stand on ethanol?

Take Bob Dole. Here's a guy with a

problem. He's an old fart. He's been trying to make the government actually function since Richard Nixon was president. He's done it with a gimp hand, a good record in the war (WW II), a loyal wife (actually two, but who talks about the first one?), and a sense of humor about how Washington works that often gets him in trouble.

On the "negative" side, he's a Washington insider, too old at 72 to be president, **slimy as a salamander on a rock, and full of so much "special interest" slush money that he couldn't find the public interest if it flashed in neon in the Lincoln Memorial Reflecting Pool.**

On the positive side, he's the majority leader of the Senate (a post last held successfully by Lyndon Johnson), the man who has brokered every successful compromise in Washington in the last 15 years, a good and wise man. But, hey, who cares?

What matters somehow -- as if Iowa matters -- is that he's not Pat Buchanan. If you like *Crossfire,* you like Pat Buchanan. You like 20-second opinions, delivered like there's some thought behind them, representing some position that somehow seems almost logical.

I like Pat Buchanan. He's my favorite asshole.

He believes what he says. And he says whatever the rich SOB's who paid his check at dinner last night tell him to say.

The thing I like about Pat Buchanan is he's a lot of fun on the campaign trail. Stump here remembers sitting in a New Hampshire restaurant in 1992 watching Pat make the rounds, shaking hands with all the reporters, having the time of his life, giving a bunch of speeches to high schools, and going down to a 63% − 37% defeat to incumbent President George Bush. It didn't really matter -- to the nation or us reporters -- that Pat Buchanan was full of shit. He was one of us.

And we are all full of shit.

We are political junkies. We are journalists who somehow think "The Nation" cares what we think. Or are we just reporting what other people say? Our conceit is that in some way America takes a plebicite on how it's doing in every presidential year. And we call that "The Campaign." We call the preliminary activities "The Primary." (Even though we -- and all our readers -- know the system is so front-loaded this year the whole thing will be over by March 19th.)

And we hunger for that moment -- during "The Presidential Debates" -- when our 30 seconds of airtime will sway the electorate to accept our opinion of what's really important. You think it's easy being a reporter? Try waiting four years at a time for a 30-second moment in the sun.

There are pundits and then there are "Pundits." And Iowa was so full of them they should have been given their own caucus. (The fact is, of course, they held the only one that mattered -- on TV.)

4

You want to know how silly it's gotten? ABC this year conducted "entrance polls" asking people how they were going to vote before they heard any of the caucus speeches. Jeff Greenfield stood in front of 80 TVs wired into 80 caucus sites and told us, "You can learn a lot from watching these." But he didn't tell us what he learned.

And then there was Cokie Roberts of ABC who, getting a jump on the pack, went off to stand in some affiliate parking lot in New Hampshire and tell us how excited she is to see the candidates arrive tomorrow (to collect the 16 Republican delegates New Hampshire will send to the Republican convention).

Are we going nuts here? Do we know any more about these candidates, their positions, the issues affecting the nation or any possible solutions? Or were we just holding a political junkie reunion so all the reporters could get together on the bus again and show off their new laptops?

When there are really major, high-level political events like "Summit Meetings," the news organizations think nothing of throwing their resources together into a single "pool reporter." Maybe we should do the same for meaningless affairs like the Iowa primary caucuses. One lone reporter travelling around with a notebook and a Hi8 camera and sending back dispatches from reality's edge. My nominee would be Jeff Greenfield, if only for that single moment when we all hover over the teletype machine to read. . . "I really learned a lot."

Mount Up! Ride to the Sound of Guns

Well, we got out of New Hampshire okay.

Bob didn't do as well as we hoped. Pat proved that 28% of the electorate will vote against anyone. And Lamar! What can I say? I love you, man.

Now let's start what we call in politics the sifting and winnowing. Let's get the kiddies off the street. Steve Forbes? Thanks for coming. It's time now to take the marbles out of your mouth and go home. Richard Lugar? You made a great mayor -- in Indianapolis -- go try again. Morry Taylor? Back to hubcap management. Alan Keyes? Who are you anyway and why are you here?

Let's get on to something important: a political primary where more than my mother's bridge club gets to vote.

Let's get to some state where you can actually BUY THE ELECTION -- someplace where you can efficiently spend enough money on television to affect enough voters to win enough delegates to the Republican convention to

6

make a difference. **Welcome, as our tourism bureau would say, to Illinois.**

Sure, you can spend as much money as you want proving you are the King of Pooh in Arizona, North Dakota, South Dakota, or South Carolina, or wherever else your pollsters say you have a snowball's chance in the next few weeks. But let's look to the future. The Illinois primary is March 19th. On the same day, they will hold primary elections in Michigan, Ohio, and Wisconsin. The next week, it will be California's turn. Inside of seven days, 392 delegates (20%) of The Republican Convention will be apportioned.

Whatever else happens in the dinky states, even before Illinois comes around, Bob Dole is sure to pick up the bulk of New York's 102 delegates March 7th (if only because Alfonse D'Amato has it wired tighter than braces on a teenager).

So where did New Hampshire leave us? I'd say in a metaphorical tie. If you go by actual delegates, New Hampshire came out Buchanan (6), Dole (4), Alexander (4), and Forbes (2). Not the kind of numbers that are going to make Steve Forbes book the Queen Elizabeth as his convention hotel or send Bob Dole running for the hills, but my guess is the old Dolester's got to be a little shaken.

"The fax machines are working overtime in Washington tonight," Pat said as he accepted his first win. "They're all out to get us. So don't wait for orders from headquarters, mount up and ride toward the sound of the guns."

7

The problem is there are guns popping all over the place. We call them political pundits. Their sound, unfortunately, obscures the fact that once out of New Hampshire, the presidential campaign takes on a whole new look and feel.

Mark Shields said it best. "There are only four elements to a campaign: Money, Message, Mechanics and Momentum. Dole's got the Money and Mechanics, but his Message is nowhere. Buchanan has a clear Message and Momentum, but no Money or Mechanics."

In the waning hours of election night in New Hampshire, I think I detected a pulse in candidate Dole. Whether out of embarrassment or shock, the front runner seems to be awakening to the fact this election is not his by divine right (especially given the predilections of the Divine Right).

He, too, knows he probably has to stand for some-thing and not just beat down his opponents with negative TV spots. Pat Buchanan is going to get 25% of the vote wherever he chooses to challenge Dole, and he has chosen to challenge him everywhere. He's going to get 25% in his good states, and 25% in his bad states because Pat Buchanan represents 25% of America -- the ugly part.

What Bob Dole has to come up with is a position that convinces the other 75% of the moderate Republicans he has more brains than some guy who calls himself Lamar!

Okay, no more jokes about the ex-governor from Tennessee who leans too close to the camera, wears red plaid shirts, and used to play piano for The Billy Graham Crusade. (Can anybody here say Jimmy Carter?) This could be "The Best Man The Republican Party" has to offer.

In a three-way race, we've got a little time to let Bob and Lamar! wrangle for the heart and soul of The Republican Party, as Bob put it. And if Bob is going to go the distance, he should have to prove himself against someone besides The Millionaire, The Kook, The Tire Magnate, and The Hoosier.

Bob Dole is a long distance runner.

You can con him, stunt him, spit on him, or anything else you want to do, but he ain't going to quit. And you aren't going to beat him. You don't have enough money.

The suspicion is growing that as lame as Lamar! is on television, his voice is starting to cut through and, if Bob begins to falter, The Money will come swinging his way.

We got a couple weeks now for the pundits to sort out this mess The Republicans have gotten themselves into and, occasionally, we'll probably let a few voters cast their ballots.

But from here on in, this is **A Money Game**. And no one's better at money than Bob Dole -- except Bill Clinton. Bring him on.

If a Tree Falls In the Desert?

If a tree falls in the desert, will any- body hear?

They will if it knocks down 39 delegates in a single winner-take-all primary. And they will if it's conducted, for the first time in a millenium, in a territory we call -- Arizona.

Ah, the home of Barry Goldwater, what better place for America to celebrate the roots of American conservatism? You remember Barry Goldwater? **The guy in** Scottsdale whose house has an electronic flag pole that raises and lowers Old Glory at 9 AM and 5 PM on the digital dot.

The guy who blew his daddy off the toilet

at the age of 12 with a cherry bomb? The guy who ran for president in 1964 on the motto "I'd rather be right than President"? The guy who told Richard Nixon to go away, we don't need you anymore?

The 87-year-old patriarch of conservatism -- the author of *The Conscience of a Conservative* -- who asked a young man named Pat Buchanan to write the introduction back in 1960?

If Pat Buchanan was going to win the Republican nomination, Arizona should have been his springboard. He worked hard to win it, sniping at immigrants, holding rifles over his head, talking about a revolution in Washington.

Too bad for Pat that Goldwater, now mellow in his old age, thinks he's a dangerous fruitcake, and Steve Forbes, who *is* a dangerous fruitcake, spent more money than God pulling a victory out of the waterhole.

The Arizona vote was Forbes 111,000 (33%), Dole 101,000 (30%), and Buchanan 92,000 (27%).

The Good News for Forbes is that he's bringing down his cost per vote from $450 in Iowa to $200 in Delaware to $40 in Arizona. The bad news is that The Media is about to jump him.

Cokie Roberts tipped off the attack on ABC's *Good Morning America*.

"Who can stop him?" she asked. "He can spend as much money as he wants to spend. He's not taking any federal money, so he has no spending limit. And he can just keep going. If Steve Forbes decides to spend 50 million or 100 million of his dollars, who's going to stop him?"

The good news for Dole is that he's looking more alive every day. He's changed around his stump speech, fired the idiots who told him he was winning, and set his sites on Bill Clinton, who is, when all is said and done, the man the Republicans have to beat.

As he moves into the nine primaries next Tuesday (mostly in New England, but also in Georgia and Colorado), Dole's image is coming into focus. He's not the rich guy who's trying to buy the White House and he's not the right wing extremist who's trying to storm it. He's got a little room here to start defining a candidacy other Republicans might want to vote for.

The good news for Buchanan is he got to ride a buckboard in a parade, made friends with a lot of people who have guns, and was given more cowboy hats than any Irishman can fashionably wear.

And he gets to move next to South Carolina -- one of his bedrock states in the Bible-belted South -- where he ought to get 30-40% of the extremist vote while Dole and Alexander hack it out for the blah Republicans.

The beauty of the Arizona primary is the meaninglessness of it all. I checked in on the *Buzz* column on my favorite internet service, PoliticsUSA, and discovered that prior to yesterday, there was no such thing as an Arizona presidential primary.

Arizona Senator John McCain and Governor Fife Symington -- both ardent supporters of former candidate Phil Gramm (R-Texas) -- decided last year that they could help their guy by creating a "first in the west" primary. Originally, they thought they could pre-empt New Hampshire's claim to the first in the nation status, but when Gramm told them they were dumb as a stump (media-wise) they slipped it back a week. (And then those slimes in Delaware snuck in.)

What's interesting about Arizona -- aside from the unrelenting niceness of the place -- is that it's a lot like California (which holds its primary on March 26th). It's a western state -- a good-weather state -- with a lot of snowbirds, optimistic people, and cheap labor that comes across the border from Mexico to serve their needs. Pat Buchanan's Mexico bashing didn't play well here. That does not bode well for the increasingly important California primary.

If you get back to the meaning of Arizona, it means that deserts in America count. You grab a river like The Colorado, dam it up, spread free water around the place and call it Phoenix. A bunch of people go there because it's warm in the winter and presto! you have a population center. You buy two media markets -- Phoenix and Tucson -- for $3 million -- and presto! you are a frontrunner in the presidential race.

Is Arizona a real primary? Let's see here. The Democrats didn't even vote. (The rules of winner-take-all primaries don't jibe with Democratic convention rules so no Democrats including President Bill Clinton entered.) The state and local races don't hold their primary until September. As a result, the voter turnout was something on the order of 16%.

The Arizona Presidential Primary, as concocted by McCain and Symington, was an election no one wanted to hold. The taxpayers resented the fact it cost them $2.5 million just to open the polls. (And to keep costs down, Phoenix decided to open only 110 of the 900 usual polling places, thus giving rise to a new rule allowing anyone anywhere to vote wherever they want, as often as they want. Thus giving rise to a semi-famous quote from Arizona Democratic Chairman Sam Coppersmith, "At least in Chicago, the dead people can only vote in their home precincts.")

Old Steve Forbes is riding pretty high after Arizona. He can't expect to do all that well in South Carolina, but he spent $1 million buying his way onto the New York ballot March 7th (a feat no other contender accomplished besides Dole) and there's plenty more where that came from. Alas, however, there is a downside. New York holds to the old axiom: a fool and his money are soon parted.

Stay tuned!

Lamar! We Hardly Knew Ye

Fourth place is nothing to be ashamed of -- as I keep telling my seven-year-old -- but in presidential politics you have to cut the rope somewhere, and for Lamar Alexander, that somewhere was South Carolina.

Lamar! I still love you, man. But this waiting around for Bob Dole to stumble is one of the lamest campaigns I've seen in years.

You had your chance -- hell, we gave you two weeks to articulate a position -- and all you did was run around creating photo opportunities. Even Newt Gingrich says he wants you and Lugar out of here.

South Carolina's primary this Saturday was billed as the gateway to the South and Bob Dole took it faster than Fort Sumter. The final tally was Dole 45%, Buchanan 29%, Forbes 13%, Lamar! 10% in a race that brought out a record Republican vote.

Yes, there were only 37 delegates at stake, but Dole won them all. More important, given the battle to capture The Big Mo, he won the exit polls -- splitting the undecideds, out-pointing Buchanan for The Religious Right, and winning the coveted commentator spin hands down.

On Tuesday, when eight other primaries are held, South Carolina will be a distant memory. By Thursday, when New York weighs in, the three-way race between Dole, Buchanan, and Forbes should be pretty much set. Will Lamar! hang in? One hopes not.

The Lesson of Lamar Alexander should be that you can't run for president with no ideas. You can be nice, photogenic, optimistic, and upbeat, but pretty soon you have to stand for something.

Lamar! never quite could. (Probably because he was too busy walking.) Is there a political gimmick Lamar! didn't try? He wore plaid shirts to show he was homespun, wading boots to counteract mud-slinging, and hats touting every Shriner convention that would let him attend. In all his many travels, he never met a piano he wouldn't bang.

Even after the pasting he took in South Carolina, Lamar! didn't learn his lesson. **He ran right off to Florida for a photo-op picking up garbage in the Everglades.** Lamar's contribution to American politics this year was to give photo-ops a bad name. (Not that everyone gets it. Steve Forbes was seen the same day dancing with a cow at a New England dairy.)

We should thank Lamar! for all the good fun and waking up Bob Dole, then send him on his way. This is not a gimmick year in American politics. This is a money year. And this week will prove it.

Super, Jr.

Let's talk about something important in the Super Junior Primary: TV Graphics.

I'd have to give this one to ABC.

That 96 Vote logo spinning off the horizon is a classic. When it lands on those stars floating on the curved blue and red surface, with the big orchestra flourish, it's way impressive.

But you have to know your competition.

Call it Oppositional Research. (But pay attention!) Here are the categories:

CAMPAIGN THEME:

ABC: The 96 Vote, 3-d, gold lustre, Grand Prize.
CBS: 96 Campaign, same as always, 2nd as always.
NBC: Decision 96, 2-d, autumn yellow and blue phosphor. Traditional, but updated, a perennial 3rd.
CNN: CAMPAIGN 96 USA, 3-d, same, red, white and blue. Huh?

FLAG TREATMENT:

ABC: stars floating slowly on curvilinear globe top.
      layer 4 and 5, total layers: 6.
CBS: stars floating flat into the horizon
      ("long ago in a galaxy far away. . .")
      layer 4, total layers: 5.
NBC: furling and unfurling in lower right and lower left
      corners. layer 1, total layers: 5.
CNN: stars flying in meteor shower, red bar, white let-
      tering. layers, all, total layers: 8
      (also furling on top to intro the graphic.)

FLAG COLORATION:

ABC: muted red & blue
CBS: muted red & blue
NBC: red, white & blue
CNN: red, white & soft blue

THEME MUSIC:

ABC: Aaron Copland knock-off
CBS: battlefield drums ("When Johnny Comes Marching Home")
NBC: kettle drums
CNN: Aaron Copland knock-off

MAP MOVEMENT FOR WINNERS:

ABC: 2-d color high-lighted states
CBS: states rise in 3-d
NBC: not determinable
CNN: 3-d map morphs into individual states

RESULTS (aka ELECTION RETURNS)

basic colors:

ABC: red, white & blue
CBS: red, white & blue
NBC: autumn yellow & blue phosphor
CNN: red, white & blue

PROJECTED WINNERS:
Flashing, Check mark, Blinking?

ABC: yes, yes, no
CBS: no, yes, no
NBC: yes, yes, yes
CNN: no, yes, yes

WHICH IS BIGGER:
Check mark, winner percentage, total votes, delegate
totals, percentage of precincts reporting?

ABC: check mark
CBS: winner percentage
NBC: winner percentage
CNN: check mark

TRANSITION BETWEEN RESULTS:

ABC: mosaic wipe
CBS: page peel
NBC: window-shade wipe
CNN: door-close wipe

DISCLAIMER AT BOTTOM:
(percentage of vote reporting),(point size/visibility)

ABC: none
CBS: 18 pt., light
NBC: 24 pt., moderate
CNN: 24 pt., moderate

NETWORK ID:

ABC: The 96 Vote animation
CBS: 96 Campaign animation
NBC: Blow-You-Away-Hip Graphic Look (and also live from
     Tampa, Florida...) teased between *Frasier* and *The
     John Laroquette Show.*
CNN: Push into presidential seal reveals CNN logo.

FACE TIME:

ABC: Peter Jennings, Ted Koppel, Lynn Sheer (pollster),
     Hal Bruno (political analyst), Jim Wooten, Jeff
     Greenfield, Cokie Roberts.
NBC: Tom Brokaw, Tim Russert.
CBS: Dan Rather
CNN: Judy Woodruff, Bernard Shaw, Kellyanne Fitzpatrick
     (political analyst), Ken Bode, William Schneider
     (pollster).

ANCHOR BACKDROP:

CBS: Studio
NBC: Graphic -- composited layers of flag.
ABC: Studio (You won't believe this one. They made Lynn
      Sheer go stand in "virtual set" blue screen cubicle
      for a walk-on-top-of-the-map-and-talk-at-the-same-
      time-reading-from-cue-cards-shot-while-pointing-at-
      things-I-can't-see-just-like-a-weatherman-does,
      just because they could.) And like -- me to you --
      it stunk.
CNN: Around a table in "The Den."

THE LEAD:

ABC: a clean sweep for Dole.
NBC: a clean sweep for Dole.
CBS: a clean sweep for Dole.
CNN: a clean sweep for Dole.

Dole On a Roll

The Bob Dole juggernaut -- if you can call it that -- rolled through New York last night, capping off a big week of primary victories for the Man from Kansas.

The great minds who are handicapping this race probably won't be put off by the fact Dole's win came in a New York primary held on the wrong day, in bad weather, in an election that was rigged from the get-go.

Bob got his 102 delegates -- a clean sweep. He can claim he's won 10 primaries in a row this week. But someone in the Dole camp ought to be a little concerned that Dole won New York with less than 8% of the registered Republican voters; confirming, as one pollster put it, **"The enthusiasm level of his supporters is a little less than you'd want to see."**

That is to say, Bob won New York the way Bush won Somalia or Clinton won Haiti -- by showing up.

Who else could have won? Pat Buchanan? Even if his name were on the ballot in all Congressional districts, Buchanan is not a New York type guy. Steve Forbes? He toyed with the idea. He spent a million to get on the ballot and another million on a 5-day TV buy, but you can't toy with the presidency. You have to run for it, and Stevereno just doesn't seem to have the legs.

In the end, Dole gathered slightly more than 200,000 of the 400,000 votes cast (out of 2.8 million registered Republicans) -- a hum-drum victory at best. So where does that leave Bob Dole? Back out front where, as they say, it's the one you don't hear that gets you.

In a remarkable sort of way, this primary season is going just the way the Dole campaign planned it. Sure it was hard to rev up the old guy to take to the stump again, but the campaign has now moved quickly from "retail campaigning" -- where you go after votes one handshake at a time -- to "wholesale campaigning" where one good TV spot can swing eight states in a day.

Dole was never good in the one-on-one meet the voters. He bombed in Iowa, New Hampshire, and South Carolina in 1988 and, if you measure total votes then and now, he didn't do much better this year. But the Dole strategy was always to bull it out through the early primaries, then crush them with organization and money in the South on Super Tuesday, the Rust Belt the next week, and California March 26th.

In the wholesale stage of delegate hunting, Dole can once again fall back into the 72-year-old patrician that

he is. No more riding around from Plainfield to Mudville
with the boys on the bus in New Hampshire. Goodbye
Christian Coalition and all your little rallies for life
in South Carolina church basement gymnasiums.

In this phase of the primary season, we're back on the 747, dropping down in Cleveland for lunch, Detroit for dinner, with an overnight in Chicago after a $1,000-a-plate fundraiser at the Hyatt. This is Bob Dole's kind of campaign.

We're now entering Republican Lent, where the party
faithful give up thinking and select 63% of all the
Republican delegates to the San Diego Convention. The
whole primary season is so crammed into these 31 days of
March, that only a candidate with a national organization and lots of money can handle the logistics. You
think this is an accident? Primary dates are set by each
state, and 31 of the 50 states have Republican governors.
Two dozen of them support Bob Dole.

In 1992, if you remember, Clinton had to slug it
out with Paul Tsongas and Jerry Brown from February in
New Hampshire to June in California in a conga line of
contests that swung Tuesday to Tuesday from The South to
The Midwest to The West, back to New York, over to
Pennsylvania, and finally into New Jersey and California.

Every week gave rise to a new controversy -- Gennifer Flowers, Whitewater, The Draft -- and Clinton had to beat them back, one week at a time, at an ultimate cost of $25 million (and not a little personal embarrassment).

Bob Dole would have died in the first lap running around a track like that. So the party leadership, which is more and more falling into the hands of governors, **telescoped the process to be over by the end of March,** so the winner could rest up for the big race in the fall.

Dole's big win in New York wasn't against his opponents, but the media.

Remember how the New York tabloids -- the *New York Post,* in particular -- ate Clinton for lunch in 1992. They didn't lay a glove on Dole this year because. . . face it, there wasn't enough time.

Events are rolling along so fast from South Carolina to Junior Tuesday to New York Thursday that Dole went from dead to unbeatable to *adios amigos* before the New York papers could re-plate.

Now that Dole has escaped the snake-pit of the New York tabloids, the burden falls on what remains of The Boys on The Bus, those Arthur Kroch wannabees who dog the presidential trail looking for insight and revelation to pull Dole out of the cushion of campaign handlers who protect him from answering for himself, and make him answer to the question: Why are you doing what you do?

Where are the nit-pickers in this crowd? Who's asking Dole the hard questions? How come Ted Koppel can't even get him onto *Nightline?* **Where are the nattering nabobs of negativism when we need them?**

What questions are they supposed to ask?

Well hell, let's start with this one: **If you're such a shrewd budget dealmaker in Washington, how come we're three months into the new year and you can't get a federal budget passed?**

Is President Clinton so intractable or is it because you can't control The Junior Newt who's holding the House captive?

And if you're such a leader, how will you handle the contentious freshmen Republicans in the House? And what is the Republican vision for Bosnia? And how strongly will you, once president, campaign to get that Constitutional amendment banning abortion?

No one is going to trip Bob Dole up on his personal habits.(I was going to say "catch Bob Dole dead in the bed of a bimbo," but, of course, that's probably exactly how they'd catch him.)

But there are very real questions to be asked about whether he isn't so old and so set in his accomodating ways that he won't become the weakest Republican President since Andrew Johnson.

The Dole machine is rolling along nicely into Super Tuesday just slighly ahead of schedule. Bob's Boys have the three-way race they wanted. Gramm, Lugar, and Alexander are out of the picture. Buchanan is sputtering on the right and Steve Forbes is becoming the Rollie Rich Kid everyone loves to hate.

This coming Tuesday, Dole doesn't have to win most of the southern primaries, he has to win all of them. If he doesn't, he'll let Buchanan back up off the mat. And that could bring on a Pat revival in Michigan, a Forbes challenge in California, and a prolonged internecine battle lasting right into the convention.

"We go to San Diego. We break the doors open to this party, and we take it over," Pat vowed last night in New York.

Battlin' Bob's got to put this baby to bed because the longer it goes on, the weaker he'll get.

And his face shall grow weary, and his eyes shall grow wan, and the sharks in the press shall rise to the smell of his blood.

The Talk of Naperville

I was sitting with Lucy's Mother, sewing buttons on garments headed to a New York fashion show, when she began to talk -- finally -- to me.

It was a Friday evening, and she had just come from a long hearing to obtain a residential nursing license for a company that relied on Medicare repayments to exist, which required a certificate for resident nursing licensing from the Illinois Bureau of Professional Certification, which then triggered -- if the government actually happened to be writing checks -- a repayment for services rendered (at 90% of the going rate last year, thank you Newt Gingrich) for Social Security recipients who were soon going to die.

"Medicare and Medicaid, I think they're all going away," Lucy's Mother said. "No one cares about the cost of health care these days."

"So you like being a nurse?" I asked.

"I used to be a nurse. Now I'm a health-care manager. I supervise nurses and do training. I used to work for a big company where I trained nurses but then I joined this new company where there are only four of us now, but we can't get started until we get the Medicare certificate," she said.

"So I hear you bought a new condo in Naperville, "I said.

"It's not actually in Naperville. It's four miles away in Lisle. You wouldn't believe what a difference it makes. It's not like it's the rich part of town or any-thing, but it's a lot quieter. Downtown Naperville is like living at Clark and Division. Sirens all the time and no parking. The suburbs are becoming like the city. But Lisle is different."

"Is that bad?" I asked.

"No, I kind of like it. I'm used to small towns," she said.

"Who do you like in this Republican Thing?" I asked.

"I'm not a political person."

"Did you vote?" I asked. "Who did you vote for?"

"I don't remember," she said. "I'm not a politi-cal person."

"So you must like someone? Dole? Forbes? Buchanan? Alexander?"

"Buchanan? Isn't that the guy on Channel 38?" she said.

"No, that's Pat Robertson. He ran for president in 1988," I said.

"Well, they all kind of look the same. I don't pay much attention . . . but I used to be political. I was a member of the League of Women Voters in Rockford, I did volunteer voter registration. . . . Then. . . I don't know, when Lyndon Johnson just kept that war going after everyone, even me, could see it was wrong. . . I kind of lost interest in politics."

"So did you vote for George McGovern in 1972? Jimmy Carter? Ronald Reagan? George Bush? Bill Clinton? Did you ever vote for a guy who won?"

"Bill Clinton," she said. "I remember I voted for Bill Clinton. . . and you know something? Hillary was right."

"About what?" I asked.

"Health care. She was right about the whole thing. The way it works. No one listened," she said. "But Hillary knew what she was talking about."

"Are you going to vote for Clinton again?" I asked.

"I'll vote for Hillary," she said, "if he doesn't abandon her."

"I believe Bill Clinton will discover Hillary is the greatest asset he has in life," I said.

"I don't know. I'm not political," she said.

(TO BE CONTINUED)

The New Precinct Captains

Bill Daley, the son of the late Chicago mayor, and a key Democratic strategist, was talking with Michael Kelly in *The New Yorker* this week about the decline of political organizations.

"The politicians can't deliver the vote anymore, because there are very few politicans who have political organizations anymore," Daley said. "Do you think you can get somebody to go out and walk a precinct anymore? Go to the front door and say, 'Hello, my name is Bill Daley, and I'd like to come in and talk to you about the election'? No way. People tell you they're going to walk a precinct, they mean they're going to stuff mailboxes. That's it. They bring their kids along, even. And that's here -- that's in Chicago. What do you think it's like in Des Moines, all due respect to Des Moines?"

The precinct captain is a time-honored tradition in Chicago, misunderstood through much of the rest of the country. People seem to still believe the precinct captain in Chicago gets you an extra garbage can in the alley, or a job down at The Hall or a permit for that awning you want to hang over the sidewalk. The fact is your alderman does that. **What your precinct captain does, as Daley rightly points out, is knock on your door and "come in to talk to you about the election."**

In this era of reduced leisure time, fewer volunteers are ringing the bell and fewer still are getting in the door. But since politics is such a fascinating topic, our interest in chewing over the events of the day is not diminished but displaced to the new precinct captains, who come into our homes through the door we always leave open, our television sets.

It's not a new thought that the political commentators on TV and radio are America's electronic precinct captains. Dan Rather, Peter Jennings, and Tom Brokaw would gladly accept the mantle and any number of radio talk show hosts actually aspire to it. But I think they overrate their own importance.

The TV news anchors, as they are used in today's election coverage, are merely the glue holding together staccato reports from the field, and, as much as radio talk show hosts can pepper the airwaves with their opinions, nobody really trusts a radio talk show host, and you certainly wouldn't invite one into your home.

A good precinct captain is someone you invite into your home because you want to know what he or she has to say. He's the helpful neighbor, the jovial scout leader or the guy at the corner tap with all the time in the world, and all the opinions. There are certain archtypes, and yes they do exist on television today, but their influence derives less from their position in the media than the style in which they deliver their message.

America's Number One precinct captain is Ted Koppel.

No one forces us to watch another half-hour of news after the 10 o'clock news, but millions of us tune in *Nightline* every night to see Koppel discern and dissect the issues of the day. His avuncular opening -- always ending with a question: "Is Bob Dole winding down his primary run or are his troubles just beginning?" -- promises us an evening of chew and flap we can nod along to, or just fall asleep on.

Koppel's approach is to treat every political contest as a civics lesson. He is like the high school social studies teacher who works for the Democratic Party on the side. We are surprised when he shows us his partisanship, but not disapproving because he is merely putting his principles into action.

Equally effective, in a totally different way, is Rush Limbaugh. He is The Republican Captain of the Air, the "hail fellow well met" who sits by the cracker barrel telling jokes around the hot stove about those idiots back in Washington. His humor is infectious, his arguments so flabby as to be incontrovertible and his appeal for your vote so subtle, you've nodded five times before you realize, "This guy is not making any sense."

In the daytime precincts, Oprah Winfrey rules the roost. She's your neighbor coming by in the morning for girl talk in the kitchen over coffee, and when she brings her favorite candidate along, you'll listen. Oprah's influence is so great precisely because she seems non-political. So much of her show is about lifestyles, we hardly question when she brings politics into the mix.

In the evening, Oprah's night-time counterpart is Larry King. He is a throwback, a Walter Winchell for the grey hairs who remember when show business was show business. If Larry takes a liking to you, his audience is yours; and if he doesn't, you'll never darken his doorstep again. In the cloak of Larry's celebrity, politicians become celebrities and we, lucky us, can meet them right there on *Larry King Live!*

The precinct captains who influence us most are ostensibly the least political of all, Jay Leno and David Letterman, who choose their candidates based on joke-appeal.

I've had precinct captains like that. People who I've laughed along with for months before realizing my whole political view was shaped by their humor. Although I would hardly want Leno or Letterman invited to the White House, I'd hang on their every word after they left.

The effective precinct captain never pushes the hard sell. First, he befriends you. Then he entertains you. Finally, as he is leaving, he will just slide the literature over on some side table for you to look at when you get a chance.

Between them, Koppel, Limbaugh, Winfrey, King, Leno, and Letterman cover all the precincts of television -- daytime, afternoon, prime time and late night. They may not define the hard-core issues that divide Republicans and Democrats, but their influence is enormous. They have our attention, our interest and our living rooms under their control.

If you watch closely this election season, you will know when the race is getting serious because our precinct captains will start bringing their candidates around.

Where's the 20 Mil, Phil?

One of the beauties of this here internet is that the government is in on it.

No more rooting around Washington trying to find a clerk who's not at lunch. No filling out Freedom of Information forms to read some report you saw in the newspaper. A government that actually works? This could be a dangerous thing -- especially if your name is Phil Gramm.

Phil Gramm was Mr. El Foldo in the early presidential race.

A conservative Texas Senator who made a living bashing federal spending, he raised $25 million to make the run, lost big in Louisiana and Iowa, then dropped out in February without winning a single delegate.

You don't hear much about Phil these days. He's back in Washington helping to not pass a federal budget. But you can learn a lot about Phil by dialing in the Federal Election Commission (http://www.fec.com) and reading his campaign committee reports.

At the start of this campaign, Phil was considered one of the stronger Republican contenders. He was a Texas Democrat turned Republican, a man with a thousand friends (mostly rich) who, as of the latest January 31, 1996, report to the FEC, had amassed $25,715,538 for his presidential campaign. This included $15,648,123 in individual contributions, $4,782,085 he transferred from his prior year election funds, and $3,987,412 we, the taxpayers, actually gave him from our IRS Election Fund check-off program.

Which brings me to my point: can we get our money back?

I wrote away to the FEC for Phil's expenditure report to find out how he actually spent the $25 mil. About a week later, the report landed on my desk -- all 1,750 pages -- outlining how a modern presidential campaign is conducted in America today.

The first thing you notice is that you can't run for President without talking on the phone.

Lump sum payments to AT&T and the other Baby Bells came to over $300,000 between October and the end of December, 1996. But they were only the tip of the iceberg compared to "telephone reimbursement costs" billed to the campaign by various other volunteers and consultants.

You also cannot run for President without flying around on airplanes.

As it turns out, Phil never met an airplane he
didn't love. He started out in October forking over
$211,500 to American Airlines for a raft of undated
tickets and upped the ante another $56,000 in January
when the real race started to develop. But commercial
airlines are so. . . common.

Phil Gramm's campaign really ran on private charter
jets. The records show everyone from Alpha Aviation in
Fort Worth, Texas, to The Waffle House in Norcross,
Georgia, got money from Phil for private airplanes --
over $285,000, to be exact.

**What's interesting about Phil's private air
force is how many planes were provided by his
friends in Corporate America.**

Although federal law requires reimbursement (at
the level of a first class commercial air ticket), and
Phil dutifully reported his payments, his private air
fleet included corporate planes from Hunt Oil Company,
Fisher-Scientific, AFLAC, American Home Products, U.S.
Tobacco, Spears Manufacturing, Interstate Equipment
Leasing, American Fiber & Finishing, American European
Corp, Industrial Belting & Supply, Contran
Corporation, Fibrebond, Houston Industries, and the
Triton Energy Corporation.

**Think about it for a minute. Can a guy who can pick
up the phone and hop a jet to Anywhere-In-America provided
by any one of a hundred Fortune 500 companies actually
be objective when the costs of their landing fees at National
Airport is about to be federally determined?**

Consider this: According to *Business Week*, the Glaxo, Ltd. Pharmaceutical company is flogging a special patent extension in the Senate this month for their ulcer remedy Zantac and other brand name drugs. If it passes, Glaxo will be the chief beneficiary of an estimated $2.5 billion in additional sales.

At the same time the Senate is considering the bill, Phil is joyriding around in his presidential quest on a Glaxo jet (and reimburing them $588.)

Watch the Senate this month to see just how cheap a Senator comes these days in America.

Like most campaigns, Phil needed a campaign staff, and he put together a doozy.

He accumulated a network of payrollers and consultants, in Washington, D.C. and around the country, that makes The Dole Organization look mean and lean.

In key states, Phil rented headquarters and hired local consultants early in October 1995, who drew monthly retainers, plus expenses, through January 31, 1996.

The modus operendi was $3,000 a month rent and $4,500-$6,000 a month consulting fees (memo to Jeanne Flaherty, Fargo, N.D.: you got gypped at $1,500 flat.)

But the biggest payouts in the Gramm Campaign were reserved for the high-rolling political consultants in Alexandria, Virginia, and his native Texas, who handled the polling, direct mail, and media buy for the campaign.

For polling alone, Gramm gave Linda DiVall and her American Viewpoint Consulting $184,000. For TV and other advertising, Phil gave National Media, Inc. of Alexandria $1,586,000 (before the first primary was even held). He threw $56,000 to Charlie Black and his Huckaby & Associates, $52,000 to Nancy P. Hubbard & Associates, and $20,000 to something called Washington Communications, which, of course, is located in . . . you guessed it. . . Alexandria, Virginia.

The big winner was Gramm's old crony John D. Weaver of San Antonio, and Weaver's Campaign Services Group in Austin, Texas. Weaver turns out to be the Wonder Boy of Campaign '96, the point man in a direct mail campaign that, in effect, became a self-amortizing fundraising appeal that made the whole Gramm For President effort possible.

From October through January, the Gramm Organization gave The Campaign Services Group $706,360 for printing, postage, and the direct mail of fundraising appeals to the conservative bastions of the Republican party. But this was only a start.

They also gave Mail America, another right wing direct mail outfit, $172,200, RST Marketing $112,500, Highland Technologies (in Baltimore) $48,000, and Mail Marketing Strategies (in South Carolina) $20,230.

Overall, Gramm's itemized costs for all direct mail expenses came to $1,854,000. This included $476,000 for postage, $200,000 for acquisition of mailing lists, and $120,000 for just the mechanical side of processing, labelling, folding, stuffing, and getting out the junk.

The sad fact is the vast majority of these mailings were not designed to solicit a single vote, but rather to raise the bulk of the $16 million that **the federal government then matched -- at a rate of $250 for every $1,000 -- to finance Gramm's 1996 campaign.**

Spend $1.8 million to raise $16 million that is matched by a guarantee of $4 million from the Federal Election Commission?

Not a bad scam. No wonder eight people jumped into the Republican primaries. **Phil Gramm proved there's money to be made running for president, and you can have quite a ride doing it.**

The 1,750 pages of Phil's campaign report is a wealth of trivial information. Under "list acquisition," for instance, Gramm reported giving the Arizona Republican Party $6,394 for its mailing list and the Iowa Christian Coalition $14,000 for its list.

Are there really more Christians in Iowa than Republicans in Arizona, or was Phil just buying off a key voting bloc?

And what about that $125,000 party Phil threw in Orlando last November? Just kicking out the winter blues? Hardly. The weekend of November 15th was the date of the Florida Republican straw poll, also known as "Presidency III," where 3,400 Republican gathered to hear the candidates and cast sample ballots.

Phil was right there in the middle of them. CNN's

Gene Randall reported that Gramm, ". . . in an effort to shift his campaign out of neutral,"went around the convention accusing Bob Dole of everything from buying delegates Godiva chocolates to giving them free hotel rooms.

Well, Phil ought to know.

His campaign reports show he gave the Omni Rosen Hotel in Orlando $76,000 for "event expenses" that weekend and spent an additional $42,308 for "lodging" at the Stouffer Rennaissance. And what did he get for his efforts -- 869 meaningless votes (26%), and second place. At a cost per vote that makes Steve Forbes look frugal.

Is there a trick in the campaign books that Phil missed?

Phone banks? No, sirree. He dropped $134,000 on a California company called Contact America to hit his voters in December and January, hired Per Mar Security Services of Davenport, Iowa, to blanket the caucus state for another $69,000, and spent $9,000 on oppositional research from The Luntz Research Company.

Web site? Got it covered through Berkeley Internet Connections.

Door-to-Door? Who needs to talk to the people when they're rich?

The Phil Gramm Campaign was a textbook case in American Politics, spending $20 million and gaining not a single delegate vote -- eclipsing the old $12-million-for-one-delegate record previously held by fellow Texan John Connally.

The only good thing you can say about his campaign is that Gramm left the race with $5 million in unspent money -- a good start for his Senate re-election campaign in Texas.

Now some may argue this is not real tax money, just the accumulated dollars we voters voluntarily check off on our tax returns to finance presidential campaigns.

Which only goes to show, if there's a bigger fool in America than Phil Gramm, it's us.

On Vacation

A day without Stump is like a day without sunshine. Let me tell you about it.

I lost my Powerbook the other day. I sent it in to Repair and they told me I had a faulty logic board that would take ten business days to replace. So I went on vacation. Why the hell not?

Well, let me tell you, vacation was crowded.

Every day I picked up the newspaper, there was Bob Dole lounging around his retirement condo in Miami, and Bill and Hillary traipsing around Korea, Japan and Russia, giving the presidential shoulder hug.

If I have to read one more article about Dole's poolside reading, Blockbuster video choice, T-shirt, caps, thighs. . . thighs? . . . well, let me tell you, at least my vacation was a serious one.

I went to Las Vegas, the Day's Inn to be exact, to do my own poolside reading. The papers were pretty darn light. The *Los Angeles Times* weighed in with a long nosebleed "Is Cynicism Poisoning the Reporting of News" about the new hostile tone of the political press. In sum and substance, without recapping the whole damn 14,000 words, the article seems to follow James Fallows' argument that cynicism is poisoning the news.

44

For proof, you could read Calvin Trillin's aforementioned essay on Dole's thighs in *Time* magazine, or the *New York Times* story, buried in the back politics section, mentioning that Pat Buchanan was abandoning his presidential quest, and won't run as a third party candidate.

Fortunately, Michael Kelly of *The New Yorker* -- fast becoming my favorite political reporter -- came up with an interesting connection between Ross Perot's Reform Party and various left wing third parties -- the Green Party (started by Ralph Nader), the New Party, and Lenora Fulani's New Alliance Party. Divided by every kind of ideological issue, they are now apparently uniting under the banner of Kookdom to put a third party on all the state ballots in the fall.

For light reading (and sadistically close to the bone reality), let me be the last to recommend *Primary Colors* by Anonymous, the thinly-veiled fictional account of the Clinton campaign in 1992. All the old gang is in there -- James Carville, Susan Thomases, Betsy Wright, David Wilhelm, Mandy Gruenwald, Robert Reich, the FOB's -- and it brought a tear to my eye thinking about how much fun we all had romping around in the wake of Bill's cigarette boat, *Monkey Business II*.

I think the book kind of shorted the Illinois Primary -- the crowning achievement of the campaign -- but then, I didn't see Joe Klein here but once that week. I guess he was home writing up his notes.

Just when I thought it was safe to venture out into the casinos, the National Association of Broadcasters showed up. And who came with them? Al Gore. It's been a while since I've seen Al and, let me tell you, this VP has really beefed up. **Message to Al: time to hit the Stairmaster.**

True to form, Al didn't really say anything to stir the juices. He made a few remarks about the importance of childrens' TV, censorship on the internet, and the weather in our Capital. But he made them in the usual drone so you wouldn't miss any zzzz's listening. ("Some people think I'm stiff," Al quipped, "but they haven't gone through a winter in Washington.")

When a vice president comes to visit you on vacation, you know it's time to go home. I apologize to all my fans about leaving them with the last slander on Phil Gramm's soul. But my fans will understand and Phil Gramm has no soul. So what does it matter?

Stump is back. And so are Bill and Bob. (Can't tell you where Al is these days.) So let the campaign begin. Talk's cheap. Let's race!

The Pennsylvania Avenue Primary

After a shortened primary season -- and a few not very well deserved weeks of rest -- Bob Dole returned to the Capitol in April to lead the Republican Congress in an assault up Pennsylvania Avenue on the Bill Clinton-occupied White House.

Just when you think you've found your way back to the frontline, they end the battle. War is like that. Hell.

From a historical perspective, the pundits told us we were to witness a first in American politics: a Senate Majority Leader, the prospective Republican nominee, squared off against an incumbent President, the certain Democratic nominee, in a legislative tug of war over the central issue of our time -- how to fund and operate the federal government.

Twenty-five years ago, Eric Redman wrote an enlightening book on the process called *The Dance of Legislation* in which he outlined the many compromises, committee sessions, negotiations, and special interest tradeoffs that bring about, first, House and Senate agreement on a bill, and second, Presidential assent to sign it.

Although the process is essentially the same, the way it has played out in this election year borders on ludicrous. Returning from spring vacation, Congress really had only one significant issue before it -- nego- tiating a budget to operate the government for a year that was already two-thirds over.

Through a series of plots and ploys that included furloughing federal workers twice (then reimbursing them for the time they weren't working), closing the Washington Monument and Grand Canyon, and threatening to withhold Social Security checks at the end of January, the Republican Congress and Democratic White House bick- ered their way into The Battle of The Budget.

Bickering may be the wrong word. **The 1996 Federal Budget includes $1,600 billion ". . .to establish justice, insure domestic tranquillity, provide for the common defense, promote the general welfare, and secure the blessings of liberty to ourselves and our posterity," as Thomas Jefferson so eloquently put it.**

You'd think reasonable men could divvy up $1,600 billion without fighting over it. But, of course, we're not talking about reasonable men. We're talking Congress. To Congress, an unpassed federal budget, eight months late in the delivery, means the pork barrel is open.

And to the President it means, if you can find the right pivot point in the debate, you can be nine clicks ahead on the tracking polls come November 5th -- even with a 5% margin of error -- and who cares who gets the money?

For a while there, the Republicans let old Newt carry the ball. It was Newt and his 73 freshmen Republicans in the House who caused this standoff in the first place. It was his Contract with America (even though I, Stump, good American that I am, don't remember signing it) and his petulant refusal to sign the first budget accord -- last December -- that led to the first closure of federal offices.

By all rights, Newt *should* be carrying the ball. He was the poster boy of the Republican Revolution after the '94 elections brought Republican majorities to the House and Senate for the first time in 40 years. And he was, God knows, the only real Republican leader who was walking the walk and talking the talk while Bob, Pat, Phil, Steve, and Lamar! were off memorizing the names of small towns in New Hampshire.

The only problem with having Newt lead the charge is that, with all the other leadership off running in the primaries, Newt didn't make quite so good an impression on the public. The polls on his popularity in April (a sort of political Q-rating) had him about 37% on the positives and 67% on the negatives (which put him several clicks below even journalists).

So when Dole returned from vacation, well rested after whomping three dwarfs and a Nazi, Newt was more than willing to cede command.

The problem, unfortunately, is that in Bob's absence, the discipline that makes a party work -- the

kind of discipline that is rewarded with the title
Senate Majority Leader -- had broken down. **The lunatics
were out of control. And beyond that -- scared
and out of control.**

Through the Spring, Republican Congressmen watched
their colleagues get bumped off one at a time in key
primaries like so many beer cans on a row of fenceposts.
They faced the upcoming fall elections with a new priority -- getting re-elected.

Now, one of the most interesting activities one can
undertake is to watch freshmen become sophomores. Some
grow and transform, some rebel, some drop out. In
Washington this year, when called upon to vote for the
allocation of $1,600 billion, the freshman class fell
strangely silent during the final push and shove. It is,
in some respects, always this way in final negotiations.
**The doors close, the old hands take over, and the
young turks hit the mimeo machine.**

But this year, the old guard Republicans had a special interest in letting Bob Dole lead because this was
the primary -- The Pennsylvania Avenue Primary -- where
he could show his presidential timbre. And Bob did lead,
launching his attack on the White House by driving the
first tank into the mud.

On Monday, April 15th, the first day after reconven-
ing, and tax filing day for all Americans, the Republican
Revolution decided to pass a bill requiring a two-thirds
majority of Congress in order to raise taxes. It was a
dumbly written, ill-thought-out piece of legislation that

is going nowhere, but, since nothing else was happening that day, somebody thought it was a good gambit for the 6 o'clock news.(It wasn't. It played the back pages.)

On Tuesday, April 16th, Dole's procedural miscue allowed Senate Democrats to ressurect a bill raising the minimum wage -- a move favored by 80% of Americans and opposed by the Republicans -- for an eventual floor vote.

On Thursday, April 18th, Dole hijacked an innocuous bill that would make it easier for workers to take their health insurance from job to job, and tried to stuff it with a series of amendments aimed at forcing a Clinton veto. In spite of his efforts, five Republican Senators deserted him and the legislation became law without changes.

On Sunday, April 21st, Dole went on CBS's *Face the Nation* to defend his first week back at the helm. "It's all this inside baseball stuff," he said, dismissing the apparent gaffs.

The same day, the *New York Times* editorialized:

"Instead of running the Senate like a fine machine, churning out legislative accomplisments, Mr. Dole stumbled last week through a series of fiascos that betrayed confusion and uncertainty about the direction he intends to lead his party and, if elected, the country."

On Monday, April 22nd, syndicated columnist Bob Novak wrote that Republican offices were abuzz with talk about **". . . the worst single television interview since Ted Kennedy's 1979 encounter with Roger Mudd."**

On Tuesday, April 23rd, Dole casually suggested he and President Clinton go one-on-one to resolve the budget debate. Prompted by a Clinton invitation for a "mainstream coalition" of Congressional members to sit down and negotiate a deal, Dole responded: "You mean more people bargaining? We need fewer. How about the two candidates?"

The very prospect of a Clinton-Dole summit apparently sent shivers down the spine of both campaigns because on Wednesday, April 24th, a budget deal was announced.

One day later, it passed through both houses, with Clinton getting credit for protecting environment, education and health programs, while still meeting the common goal of reduced federal expenditures.

Just like that, The Pennsylvania Primary was over and Dole's ability to play the game, even on his home court, was more in doubt than ever.

What's most interesting about this struggle is how it played "outside the Beltway." Aside from the *New York Times* and *Washington Post*, who covered it like a local news story, the rest of the media indeed glossed over the "inside baseball stuff" for more important news. (This was, after all, the week the Bulls won 72 games and Jackie O's estate went to auction.)

For the rest of us in America, the great budget fight was reduced to another battle of 30-second television commercials -- over $30 million worth -- bouncing back and forth over the airwaves.

I call 'em the "Says No" spots because both sides resorted to the crudest sort of negative blather that said, in substance, "Dole Says No" and "Clinton Says No." The Republican and Democratic parties should both be ashamed of these tactics. Real issues are being decided in Washington and both parties decide to blow 30 million bucks of TV blarney aimed at ticking the tracking polls enough to make the other guy look bad.

The Dance of Legislation has come a long way in two decades. "If you really care about policy, you can't be absent from the airwaves," Ann Lewis, Clinton's deputy campaign manager said. But 30 seconds is hardly enough time to make an argument for anything, and these spots were so blatantly political it was hard to give them any credence.

Richard Reeves, in his new book *Running in Place*, notes:

"There is a new political language in the capital: Words, names, ideas and places have been replaced by numbers. Poll numbers and dollars."

Reeves recounts the story of Clinton at his desk after going to France in 1994 for an elaborately-staged ceremony marking the 50th anniversary of D-day. "Clinton looked at the (poll) numbers, banged his desk and said: 'All that work and my approval rating went up just 1.5 percent. Can you believe it?'"

Yes, Bill, we can. And it won't go any higher until this whole silly process changes.

The Lessons of Russia

The lesson from Russia this week, given Boris Yeltsin's resurgence in the polls, is that age old American saying: It's not over 'til it's over.

The Bill and Bob Show in Washington has thankfully only 40 more days to go before Congress adjourns (according to the *New York Times*, which, thankfully, is keeping track.)

But the remarkable coincidence is there are only 37 more days before Russia goes to the polls June 16 to elect a new president (for the first time in it's 1,600 year existence).

What's the coincidence? It's that Great Powers Thing. Russia vs. America. Big Enemies for Awhile. Detente. Yeltsin Takes Over in '91. Clinton Takes Over in '92. Yeltsin Discovered to be a Drunk in '93. Newt Leads Revolution in '94. Economy Goes Down Tubes in '95. Everybody And His Brother Decides They'd Make a Better President in '96. **Only The Strong Survive.**

In only 37 more days, we will know whether Boris Yeltsin survives the challenge of Gennady Zyuganov, who would return Russia to Communism, or Grigory Yavlinsky, who would press for more democratic reforms.

On June 16th, any of the three leading contenders can wrap the election up -- among 11 contenders -- with 50% of the popular vote. If no one receives a 50% majority, the top two will go into a runoff election to be held within the following month. But before they do, much time and effort -- and media -- will go into positioning the candidates before a disparate electorate that will, like voters everywhere, vote their own self-interest.

If the election had been held five months ago, polls showed that Yeltsin would have gone down to certain defeat. His numbers last December and January -- this is not only the first presidential election, but the first attempt at public polling, so the margin of error is quite wide -- were in the range of 5%-8% against a wide open field. But today, he actually runs neck and neck in some polls with 28% against 28% for the Communist, Zyuganov, and 7%-11% for the liberal reformer, Yavlinsky. The rest of the vote is scattered among the other candidates, all eight, among them former President Mikhail Gorbachev, who holds a steady base of supporters that constitutes about 2%.

Yeltsin has done himself no favors while in public office. Beside the aforementioned alcohol problem, his unsteady hand at the helm of the rapid transformation of Russia from a socialist to a capitalist economy -- which has given rise to massive inflation, hooliganism, and rampant graft and corruption -- has left many sorry citizens in its wake. His failure to end the rebellion in Chechyna also opened the door for hardline militarists to assert the need for tighter military rule.

Zyuganov led the communist party back into popular favor with a stunning parliamentary victory last December. As the only organized political party in the country, the communists won local district elections with solid precinct work, inspired dis-spiritedness, and plain anger over the Chechyna rebellion, and Zyuganov became a sort of Newt The Communist, using his control of the parliamentary apparatus to stump for a retro-Revolution to bring back the good old days of Communist Rule.

While Yeltsin's personal popularity plummeted over the winter (during his Chechyna Debacle), the forces of liberal reform rallied around Yavlinsky, a Harvard-edu-cated economist who broke with Yeltsin over monetary reform, and actually battled with him on the floor of par-liament, which is broadcast every day on Soviet TV and watched by anyone in Moscow who cares about anything except who shot JR on *Dallas*.

Yavlinsky is, according to most western observers, the man to watch in this election. Last week, he forged an alliance with two other minor candidates that strengthens his hand in the short run, but makes it less likely he can, by throwing in with Yeltsin at the last minute, broker a Yeltsin victory in exchange for promises of a key position -- Prime Minister, for example -- in the new Yeltsin regime.

What is kind of fun about the Russian elections is the way the candidates are running. **Like scenes out of *The Last Hurrah*,** Yeltsin and Zyuganov supporters are marching through the streets ten and twenty thousand strong holding up banners and shouting out their slogans. I imagine in my mind one group of Yeltsin supporters marching down a narrow Boston alley shouting, "Skeffington, Skeffington, He's our Man!" And another group of Zyuganov supporters coming down another alley shouting, "No, No, No!"

The Russian election will be won, through no fault of their own except naivete, through good old-fashioned enthusiasm and hard work. Precinct captains working their neighborhoods with verve and excitement. Journalists preaching the dogma of their beliefs. And broadsheets from the various parties flapping as free handouts on subway platforms and blowing across plazas and causeways for unsuspecting voters to pick out of the litter.

The Russian presidential candidates use the power of political advertising at their peril. TV and radio advertising, by law, cannot begin before May 14th and must end on June 14th. And the candidates will have to actually pay for it. Public financing of presidential elections is limited. The eleven candidates have among them only 4 billion rubles ($810,000) in public money to spend on TV advertising, and less than 30 days to spend it. No candidate may receive more than $72,000, which buys him only three prime-time spots on Moscow's most popular station.

By contrast, the public election funds Russian tax-payers donate to support election campaigns amount to less than 1% -- one penny of every dollar -- Bill Clinton and Bob Dole will spend this year in government (socially-collected, read: socialist) funds to run against each other.

The Russian elections give voters a unique option we all have at one time or another craved: A chance to vote for "None of the Above." Given that 27% of the respondents in one poll said they'd vote for "Anybody but Zyuganov/The Communists" and 37% answered "Anybody but Yeltsin," None of The Above looks, at the moment, to be the leading contender.

Yes, the elections in Russia are a free-for-all. On June 16th, we'll know whether the guy we Americans deal with is Boris Yeltsin or Gennady Zyuganov or None of The Above. And if no one gets 50% of the popular vote, we'll hear even more about them in July. But that's okay.

The more you know about your enemy the better off you are. If you want to follow the ebb and flow of the campaign, I suggest you follow the web sites 1996 Russian Presidential Election, OMRI News Digest, or Dimitri Gusev's Russian Election Watch, headquartered at the University of Indiana.

If you're just a political junkie with a vague inter-est in how Russia elects its first president please tune in. If you're not, it's a good way to practice spelling unpronounceable names we're going to have to learn soon any-way, if we want to be part of a global economy.

Citizen Dole

After a day of solemn deliberation (witnessed only by a *Time* magazine photographer and anybody who saw *Nightline*), Dole has decided to give up his 35-year career in Congress to devote his energies to running full time for President.

His speech to a packed hearing room in the Senate was, according to the pundits, a pivotal moment in his campaign. Down 17% in the polls, mired in the morass of Congress -- where only 30 days ago, he planned to make his stand -- Dole showed us a new side of his personality, a public speaker who could actually speak.

Pack your bags, boys, we're moving out. Pull the old Leader Ship out of the hangar, throw another meg on the laptop. . . and don't forget the NoDoz. Bob Dole is hitting the campaign trail.

His speech, written by New York novelist Mark Helprin, proved to be the most eloquent in Dole's career.

It was so good, in fact, it deserves more than the 8-second sound bites you heard on TV:

"One of the qualities of American politics that distinguishes us from other nations," he said in one of many wonderful passages, "is that we judge our politicians as much by the manner in which they leave office as by the vigor with which they pursue it.

"You do not lay claim to the office you hold, it lays claim to you. Your obligation is to bring to it the gifts you can of labor and honesty and then to depart with grace. And my time to leave this office has come, and I will seek the Presidency with nothing to fall back on but the judgment of the people, and nowhere to go but the White House or home.

"Six times, six times, I've run for Republican leader of the United States Senate, and six times my colleagues, giving me their trust, have elected me, and I'm proud of that. So my campaign for the President is not merely about obtaining office. It's about fundamental things, consequential things, things that are real.

"My campaign is about telling the truth, it's about doing what is right, it's about electing a President who's not attracted to the glories of the office, but rather to its difficulties. It's about electing a President who, once he takes office, will keep his perspective and remain by his deepest nature and inclination one of the people.

"Therefore, as the campaign for the President begins in earnest, it is my obligation to the Senate and to the people of America to leave behind all the trappings of power, all the comfort and security. . . and I will then stand before you without office or authority, a private citizen, a Kansan, an American, just a man.

"But I will be the same man I was when I walked into the room, the same man I was yesterday and the day before, and a long time ago when I arose from my hospital bed and was permitted by the grace of God to walk again in the world. And I trust in the hard way, for little came to me except in the hard way, which is good because we have a hard task ahead of us.

"We are gaining but still behind in the polls. The press does not lean our way. And many Beltway pundits confidently dismiss my chances of victory. I do not find this disheartening, and I do not find it discouraging, for this is where I touch the ground, and it is in touching the gound in moments of difficulty that I've always found my strength.

"I have been there before, I have done it the hard way, and I will do it the hard way once again. . . ."

Sounds good, Bob. Looks bad.

But that's not your fault. **Blame The Handlers.**
Because the same guys who gave you the speech, gave you
the *Time* photographer, Newt on *Nightline*, the powder-
blue sportcoat and tassled shoes, the appearance on Don
Imus, the stock car race in South Carolina, and all the
other humilating things about to come your way.

In one turn of the wheel, Bob, you've given up all
that you have striven to achieve in Washington. For
what? To become Joe Sixpack? I don't buy it. But I'll
bet your handlers are telling you that you're killing
them out there on the 17-city tour. The Hardest Working
72-Year-Old in Politics, to borrow a phrase from The
Rolling Stones. First stop, Chicago!

He steps off the plane and suddenly Bob Dole -- only
we can call him that now, he now refers to himself as "I"
-- speaks with a teleprompter to keep him on message. He
stops "spontaneously" in a Chicago bar, The Berghoff, to
mingle with the common people (most of whom, by the way,
are lawyers from the nearby federal courts). He cavorts
with children waving flags and pulls close the wife of the
doctor who salvaged his body from war wounds he'd rather
not remember, but has been told he cannot NOT bring up.
He says things that make no sense. To people who do not care.
(The bulk of his Chicago crowd came from an accounting
seminar in the Hilton, on lunch break.)

This is not the campaign Bob Dole would have run
(if he were running the campaign) but a series of message points and photo-ops his handlers have decreed he

must make -- to become the candidate the polls tell them can win.

Ted Koppel gave Dole's resignation a nice spin. He called it Crossing The Rubicon, A Momentous Decision, The Biggest Roll of The Dice in Bob Dole's Career.

The *New York Times* was less generous. "The soon-to-be ex-Senator has taken on the debilitating task of trying to convince voters he is something he is not," Bob Herbert noted in an op-ed page analysis. "It will wear him out and make him unhappy, and there is little chance it will succeed. Bob Dole is the insider's insider, the Senate maven who can find joy in a well-crafted amendment, and who speaks not in sound bites but in a garbled legislative shorthand. He hates campaign-ing. He does not like parading himself before the people. He is a creature of Congress, revelling in its shadows, its rituals and its privileges. Bob Dole the outsider is an oxymoron."

Stump here thinks Bob just gave in to his old nemesis, practicality.

It came in the form of yet another "new" set of cam-paign insiders -- **the bright, young, smart (cut-throat) number-jugglers so prevalent in Washington these days** -- who know everything about politics, and nothing about government, as James Carville once said of himself.

They know how to read the tracking polls, what levers to pull in the press, which questions to ask the focus groups, (who to leak the info to) and all the

other things that make them invaluable in a campaign.
The only names to surface so far are John Buckley,
Bill's nephew, as the new "communications director," and
David Keane, already on Dole's staff, but seemingly more
listened to than before. (And of course, Helprin, the
writer, who ought to get a raise.) But I'm sure there
are others and I'm sure, Bob called them all together in
a meeting and said, "Okay, what are the practicalities?"

And they told him. The practical reality is there
are no photo-ops on the floor of The Senate -- except
the hole you've been standing in for the last 30 days.

The campaign war chest is down to $177,000 (out of
$37 million) and you'll eat that up in 10 days just buying
parking and donuts for all the guys sitting around HQ
doing nothing. The coverage on The Hill is depressing and
the word going around The Beltway on your battle up
Pennsylvania Avenue is "Quagmire."

We got to get you out here, Bob.

We got to get us out of here. We got to get The Campaign
out of Washington. On The Stump. Doing Something. **Put
some tics on the polls, some numbers in the bank, some
cash-ola in the coffers.** And while we're out there, we
got to get the national committee to throw $20 million of
television dirt back our way, and we got to get those
press dogs out of Georgetown, where they're just munching
your bones between lunches with the White House guys.

We got to get you some Face Time, Bob. Exposure.
Impressions. Look-sees. Good old-fashioned flesh-pressing
with the voters, like Bill and Al did four years ago.

Remember after the convention when they and their wives dressed up like Li'l Abner and Daisy Mae and drove across Tennessee in a bus? Their numbers went up 17 points. You need 17 points, Bob. It's time to hit the road.

"Me in a bus? How many days did you say?" he replies in my mind.

Okay, so not a bus. And you don't have to be a hay-seed -- sorry, I forgot you were from Kansas.

How about something that's more you? Everybody knows you're a Senator. Resign from The Senate! **Go for Broke! Risk It All! Bet The Condo!** We all know tracking polls tic up when you do something momentous.

How about resigning to become Citizen Dole going around the country to sound out the nation? We'll do a 17-city tour -- one for every tic we're down in the polls. *You can fly!* The press will love it.

Politics are an illusion and good illusions are woven by political reporters who are on the run, chasing a story and following a campaign. Not sitting in the Senate gallery listening to filibusters on the medical accounts checkoff plan. Think of it this way. It's Free TV!

Practically speaking, The Handlers were right. Bob had to do something bold and he did. He had to make the sacrifice to reap the awards. But such a sacrifice.

Bob's numbers are going to go up. His press lineage already has, and public opinion usually swims up the widest media channel. By mid-summer, with any luck at the convention, the Republican-Democrat split in the country will even out around Clinton 40%, Dole 40%, with 20% up for grabs. After the Republican convention, the government will give Dole another $60 million (taxpayer money), he'll get his level-one secret service coverage, and he'll be back in a race he's equipped to handle.

Practically speaking, Dole made the right choice. But in his heart, I don't think Bob Dole wants to leave the Senate. I don't think he even wants to run for president anymore. Dole wanted vindication for a truly lousy run at the presidency in 1988. He knew he could do better, but he had to prove it -- to himself. And he did when he knocked off the dwarfs last March in the primaries. But this decision has taken a piece out of the very heart of Bob Dole -- the place where once he held power, and now hangs his blue suits.

From now on, he must do what his Handlers tell him to do. In for a penny, in for a pound. **He must enter the maelstrom, react to the numbers, listen to the kids, and do what they say.** He must read what they write for him -- just as they wrote it. He **must wear clothes that don't fit, go places where he is uncomfortable, and display enthusiasm for things he does not like. But alas, that is the life of a common man.** And he has chosen it.

What's interesting about Dole's farewell address is how much of Dole's ambivalence resonates between the lines. I was reminded of the concession speech Illinois Senator Alan Dixon gave in 1992 the night he lost his first election in 37 years to Carol Mosely Braun. It was as much a farewell speech to his colleagues as his voters, and it echoed the pride, joy, and sense of accomplishment he felt having been a Member of The Senate. "Those glorious years," Dixon called them in such a fond and loving way. He touched the very nerve of what makes politics so viscerally exciting -- the unspeakable bond that connects the human tissue in public bodies.

Listen again to some of Dole's resignation speech. Listen to the voice of a man ready to retire.

"We judge our politicians as much by the manner in which they leave office as by the vigor with which they pursue it. . .

"Our campaign will leave Washington behind to look to America. As summer nears, I will seek the bright light and open spaces of this beautiful country, and will ask for the wise counsel of its people. . .

"And my time to leave this office has come, and I will seek the Presidency with nothing to fall back on but the judgment of the people and nowhere to go but the White House or home."

Prepare the back room, Auntie Em, when summer turns to fall, Bob Dole is coming home.

The Talk of Naperville II

Hot air balloons... Dirty dishes ...And Annie Oakley. Welcome to Naperville.

"So what's the talk of Naperville?" I asked Lucy's Mother, doing the dishes.

"I'm not in Naperville anymore. I moved to Lisle," she said. "It's only four miles away."

"So what's the talk of Lisle?"

"The 4th of July Hot Air Balloon race over in Naperville," she laughed.

"And what do you think of the new Bob Dole?"

"He's a politician doing his politics thing. He's no different."

"What do you mean?"

"Clinton. Dole. They're all politicians. They'll be what you want them to be. . . they're just playing politics, back and forth, trying to top each other. . . I can do anything you can do better, I can do anything

68

better than you. No you can't. Yes I can. . . .No you can't. . . . Yes I can. . . Yes I can, Yes I can, Yes I can. . . . That's from *Annie, Get Your Gun!* Remember?

"You think maybe this Whitewater thing is going to rear up?"

"They haven't found anything so far. And they been looking. I guess they caught this McDougall, but I can't figure out on what. And I don't know how Clinton fits in . . . . Right now, I think Clinton has it wrapped up -- unless something happens with the foreign policy. Something in Russia maybe, or Israel or Beirut, then it could all change."

"What if Ross Perot comes in?"

"Oh, he's just in it for himself. He says he can run the government better than anybody else, but he's got to run it his way, and everything is going to have to be his way, and what if he's wrong? What if I don't want to do everything his way, give him control of everything so everyone can be like him. Frankly, I don't think anybody likes him."

"So who are you going to vote for?"

"Oh, I never tell this early. I like to keep them guessing."

Ross Perot Online

"Hi, how ya doing?" Ross Perot says, shaking hands. He stops to pose for a picture. We catch up, as if catching our breath.

Ross Perot, **the man who is not running for president,** is making yet another personal appearance, this time at the American Booksellers Convention, to promote his newest book, *The Dollar Crisis, A Blueprint to Help Rebuild The American Dream,* which he has co-authored with Illinois Sen. Paul Simon.

He travels alone. Even with an entourage, he walks four paces ahead, eyes darting to both sides, a smile for whoever makes eye contact.

It is the middle of June and Perot has plenty to think about. A site for his Reform Party Convention, to be held in August, has still not been chosen. His party is on the ballot in only 14 of the 50 states and, although there is talk of some kind of internet voting during the convention to nominate the Reform Party candidate, there has been no talk of how it will work -- if at all.

"Those are details. I don't do the details,"

Perot says brushing through the aisles on his way to the next stop. "You call the office Monday. They'll tell you everything you want to know."

"Will it all be determined on Monday?" he is asked.

"Oh, it's all determined," he said. "They just aren't in the office until Monday."

Ross Perot claps an arm around my shoulder and presses on laughing. It is hard to imagine a man having more fun tweaking the tail of the federal government. His schedule calls for a press conference, an hour of book signings, an online internet chat and private interviews afterwards. He can do it all in two and a half hours if he keeps walking, and talking, and laughing, and slapping, and greetin', and teachin' because "like my daddy in Texas used to tell me, you can do anything you put your mind to."

They call Perot the wild card in this race. That, at least, is what he proved in 1992, and it made all the difference. In again, out again, in again, with a running mate named Admiral Stockdale and $60 million of his own ($3.3 billion) fortune, he pulled in 19% of the vote, pretty much handing the election over to Bill Clinton who won, 41% to 40%, over George Bush.

In the '96 race to date, Perot hasn't even been a blip on the media radar screen. The CNN/Time poll this week, for instance, the one that had the Sunday morning talk shows all a twitter, showed Clinton's lead over

Dole has been cut to 6 points -- 49% to 43% -- but voters were not even offered a Perot option.

Except for an occasional talk show appearance,
Perot has been working the Chamber of Commerce and
Kiwanis circuit in relative obscurity. Clinton and Dole
have become so consumed in their early positioning
against each other, they don't see Perot waiting in the
wings. But he's there. Every day in every way. Putting
his mind to the problem.

He enters the press conference ten minutes late,
striding confidently to the podium while Simon huffs
along behind. (Perot is 66. Simon, 74.) He and Simon have
written their *Blueprint to Help Rebuild the American
Dream* around the need for a balanced federal budget and,
to help explain it to the lazy reporters, Ross has
brought along his ever-present slide show of charts and
diagrams. He's got the "Cumulative Trade Deficit of the
United States" and the "Net Interest Paid on the National
Debt" and a "Quarterly Analysis of the Trade Deficit with
Canada and Mexico Before and After the NAFTA Agreement"
and a lot of other pie graphs and flow charts that fly by
so fast even Perot can't keep pace with the staggering
lossses accumulating on the screen. "Who's winning? Who's
losing? We're losing. To make a long story short, what
we're doing is damaging our country," he concludes.

The question and answer period (this was too much
like a classroom) begins with a question on who wrote
what. "Who wrote the lyrics and who wrote the song," as
the reporter put it.

"Senator Simon wrote the first draft, and then I went over it and we went back and forth," Perot answers. (Never mentioning the three researchers credited in the foreward with making the complex subject easier to understand.) "But I'll tell you, this book lays the whole thing out. **I had a lot of simple people read this and they say it pulls 'em from page to page.**"

Another reporter asks about Dole and Clinton's various plans for an income tax cut. "Free candy before an election," Perot jabs into the mic as Simon steps forward to answer.

"Yes, free candy before the election," Simon repeats. "Neither of the candidates is talking about fiscal responsibility, but I think what we will find as we go into this election is people want leadership, not pandering, on this issue because it is so very central to our future."

Perot waits for Simon to step away, then steps forward himself to answer. He launches into a spit-fire, rattling discourse on currency debasement that begins somewhere back in 680 A.D. with the invention of money in Persia, winds through a quote from Cicero, touches on a Scottish philosopher from 1787, compares manufacturing versus government service jobs as a contribution to the gross national product, in light of the trade deficit, and in spite of the fact manufacturing jobs are going overseas to Taiwan for 25 cents an hour, and winds up with "what even the dumbest boy in Texas knows. You don't wait until the building's on fire before you install sprinklers."

A Ross Perot discourse on the national debt is a steeplechase of campaign rhetoric. It traverses vast stretches of history, ducks in and out of numbers, leaps obstacles and incorporates pieces of minutiae that leave you marvelling over when Perot ever found time to study Scottish philosophy. Did he take the Evelyn Wood reading course? And when he talks like this, how does he remember where he started and where he's going?

In person, Perot is a kind and very likable man, both more warm and more serious than the satirists make him out to be. (His ears, contrary to popular opinion, do not flop like gills on a catfish.) He takes time at the press conference to plug his friend Joe's book *On the Brink* from the same publisher (the Summit Publishing Group of Arlington, Texas), and allows that all his royalties are going to a charity ". . . my wife will choose, probably the Salvation Army."

When the press conference is over, several reporters line up to get their copy of the book autographed. Perot signs quickly and moves out, trailing along his bodyguard, a publicist, and a spear carrier in a suit who carries under his arm the carousel of slides. "Hurry up, we can't be late for that internet thing," he says.

The internet thing is a live chat session in the *Bookweek* booth. Perot and Simon take seats next to a woman who will type in their responses. The first question is to Perot.

>The system administrator has chosen this question:

> "Do you regret having Admirable Stockdale as your running mate?"
>/blurb Perot:
>No. He is an American hero, a patriot and a scholar.

>The system administrator has chosen this question:
"Are you more concerned with private or public debt?

Simon and Perot confer, not quite knowing how to answer a long question in such a stunted format. Simon takes a stab at it in a sentence. Perot rocks back listening, then adds:

>/blurb Perot:
> Here's Ross Perot's advice on how to stay out of debt. Save your money. Don't use credit cards. Pay cash.

Perot looks over at Simon, content with himself. "I don't think a little delayed gratification hurts anyone. When I was a kid, looking forward to having something was better than getting it."

>The system administrator has chosen this question:
"What is the solution to the National Debt?"

>/blurb Simon:
> It's in the book.

>/blurb Perot:
>As the TV evangelist would say, it's in the book.

>The system administrator has chosen this question:
"Will you run again?"

>/blurb Perot:
>My job is to help the people create a new political
party. They will select the candidate. That's it.
Leave it at that.

P.S. I called the Reform Party today to find out
how the convention plans were coming. Still no site
selected. Still no word on how we are going to vote over
the internet to select our candidate. Two more states
certified the Reform Party for the ballot today. Only 34
more to go.

The Rock

Let's start a rumble. Let's pick a fight. Let's toss some dyna- mite into the old presidential ring.

Let's invite Bill Clinton and Bob Dole to the movies, buy them some popcorn, and sit them down to watch *The Rock*.

The Rock is the Sean Connery action adventure movie that opened this weekend to a $25.1 million box office -- the biggest opening for a non-animated film in Disney history. Besides Connery, it stars Nicolas Cage and Ed Harris in a Navy Seals mission to retake Alcatraz Island from a crazed military commander who is holding 81 civilians hostage and pointing poison-gas missiles at the heart of downtown San Francisco.

Judging from the first night's audience, Bill and Bob would fit right in (Bill more than Bob. I went to the late show.) and leave the theater, as did most everyone around me, in a dizzying argument over whether the excessive violence was grotesque or fun.

Bill and Bob have had quite a bit to say on the topic of movie violence. In May, 1995, Dole staked out the territory with a speech to Hollywood executives

decrying "cultural messages (that) can and do bore deep
into the hearts and minds of our impressionable young."
Clinton came back last January with not only a bully
pulpit sermon on TV violence, but an endorsement of the
V-chip to block offending programs on the emerging
interactive television.

In Dole's case, the specific target was *Natural
Born Killers* and *True Romance.* (In Clinton's, it was two
more percentage points in the polls.) So it would be
interesting to hear either weigh in on *The Rock,* a movie
so loaded up with mayhem and murder Gene Siskel calls it
"*Speed* on speed."

It is hard to keep track of just how many people
get individually murdered in the course of this film,
but it must be in the hundreds. The means of destruction
include death by fireball, impalement on a stick,
impalement on a missile, massacre in a shower, knifing,
machine-gunning, choking on a bike chain, getting your
toes shot off (in slow motion), a chemical implosion in
the mouth, an air-conditioner dropped on your head, and
any number of just plain old bang-you're-dead takeouts
of guards and mercenaries. There's also a car chase
where 50 cars, trucks, and cable cars are totally, vio-
lently trashed, but since there are no apparent
casualties, we can't count that.

The silence of both candidates on this film is
astonishing, and it would be easy to rack up their reti-
cence to the fact the public is eating this movie up. If
the crowds continue to flock to *The Rock* in the current

numbers, it will take less than 60 days for at least half of all American adults to see it. **Telling 50% of voting Americans their taste in movies stinks probably is not the best road to the White House.**

But even the Hollywood insiders would probably concede the Don Simpson-Jerry Bruckheimer team responsible for producing *The Rock* -- well-known for their excesses -- have really gone over the top this time.

Simpson-Bruckheimer would be an easy target for Dole or Clinton, except they would also have to condemn Connery, Harris, and Cage -- icons from *Apollo 13, James Bond,* and other megahits -- who's interest was more than financial (Connery is the executive producer). But that's not all that's holding them back.

Yes, *The Rock* is poundingly violent and smash-mouth like football. It's also as American as apple pie (the hero is an FBI biochemist), and **in that fine tradition of American cinema we call The War Movie.**

As young men, Dole and Clinton had a wealth of them to choose from. *Bataan, The Battle of the Bulge, The Sands of Iwo Jima, Pork Chop Hill,* and anything with John Wayne. As a child growing up in the 50's, I can remember any number of summer nights when my Uncle Wally would haul the portable TV out on the back porch, ease back into his lounger and watch hordes of Japanese soldiers run inexplicably into the rat-a-tat-tat of machine gun fire and fall in piles in front of the camera in some late night war movie on WGN.

My uncle loved his war movies. The battles that he read about in *Stars & Stripes* as an aviator during WWII became heroic in their movie re-enactments, and he wept along with Audie Murphy, scowled along with John Wayne, and burst with patriotic pride when he saw that flag a-waving through the billowing smoke on that little lump of dirt up ahead.

In the 60's, as the memories of World War II faded, my uncle was no longer Hollywood's target, I was. World War II was not in my memory bank so Hollywood re-invented it -- not as a series of battles, but a series of missions, the precursors to today's action adventure genre. Movies like *The Guns of Navaronne, Von Ryan's Express, The Dirty Dozen,* and *Where Eagles Dare* made war a glorious venture. But it was not the patriotism of the heroes that made them prevail. It was their guile and cunning (and stealthy ability to silently strangle guards with shoelaces and piano wire).

Vietnam did not contribute much to the war movie genre -- although it did spawn a vast and rich vein of anti-war movies. (Nor did it do much for patriotric flag-waving.) Fortunately, after enough time had passed, Sylvester Stallone came along with *Rambo* -- I and II -- and re-invigorated the formula for yet another new generation using action adventure galore. What *Rambo* proved was that if the killing is fast enough, raw enough and exciting enough, you don't even have to agree with the war to like the movie.

In the 80's, without any wars to glorify, our enemies became international terrorists -- faceless, emotionless, pure villains who *"Die Hard"* but not before throwing up an arsenal of high-tech weaponry.

In *The Rock,* we have another war movie disconnected from any war. If there is an enemy, it is ourselves, personified in the villain -- Ed Harris -- the crazed commander on Alcatraz, an ex-Marine commander and Congressional Medal of Honor winner who demands a $1 million reparation to the families of each of 83 American soldiers killed under his command during U.S. covert operations. It's not much of a plot, admittedly, but it is enough to take politics out of the equation -- there's something here for the left and the right -- and leaves us to judge the movie on whether the violence is excessive or, as Gene Shalit calls it, "sensational fun."

Simpson-Bruckheimer have used every trick in the book -- pyro-technics, car chases, high-tech war gizmos, frenetic camera work, rapido-editing, driving music -- to take the violence right down to the visceral level. Never mind that it's an R-rated movie (no one under 17 admitted unless accompanied by an adult), this is a kind of mind-numbing mayhem that makes a human life about as sacred as a bubblegum wrapper.

So will Dole or Clinton take to their bully pulpits to denounce it? Probably not. Because somehow, this is not a movie that undermines American values. It glorifies them.

It has heroes. It has enemies.

It's the good guys versus the bad guys, and the good guys win so everything else is excused.

The argument over the dehumanizing nature of movie violence breaks down pretty fast when you get an audience cheering the heroes on, as they were during the concluding minutes of *The Rock*. The violence that Bob Dole and Bill Clinton like to talk about is the perverse, socially-aberrant, kinky sort you find in rock videos and gangsta rap. But it doesn't exist in a vacuum. Our heroes are every bit as violent as our social deviants because, whether you are on the right or the left side of the movie spectrum, you must always remember, it's only a movie. That's Entertainment.

If Bill and Bob want to stem the tide, what can they do? They are running for president, for Christ's sake, not studio head. They're not going to decide what makes it to the silver screen, and even if they succeed in putting V-chips into every set-top TV box in America, by the time *The Rock* rolls around to broadcast television, it will have all the bite of *The Sands of Iwo Jima*.

And Uncle Wally will wake from his sleep, hearing only the bug zapper in the quiet night, and say, "Hey, who turned off my war movie?"

Abortion

Abortion is a cut and dried issue. We approach it in code words like Pro Life or Pro Choice -- both life and choice being positions one can be for -- but advocates of either side are just **Now is the time... A defining moment... If only Bob Dole could see it.** as likely to say they are Anti-Murder or Anti-Intolerance in ways that are so accusatory they leave no bridge across the divide.

Abortion is not a pretty issue to confront, but Bob Dole has stumbled into it in a way that could provide the defining moment he has looked so hard to find in this campaign. With the promise to insert a "Declaration of Tolerance" plank in the Republican platform, Dole sets the stage for a showdown with the Religious Right that could become his own chapter in *Profiles in Courage*.

Dole did not come to his tolerance position through any kind of moral conversion. He made opposition to abortion a centerpiece of his 1974 Senate campaign and on 107 of 113 subsequent Senate votes, he has opposed any extension of abortion rights to women. In bits and fits through the primary, he has made clear his personal position was, and is, vociferously anti-abortion.

But Dole also recognizes that the Republican opposition to abortion rights is a no-win proposition. Since
the Supreme Court's *Roe vs. Wade* decision in 1973, federal and state laws have recognized the Constitutional
right of a woman to terminate her pregnancy anytime
within six months of conception.

Twenty-three years of abortion on demand have led
to an average of 1.3 million to 1.6 million legal abortions a year, according to the National Center for
Disease Control, which is to say, one of every three
(33%) of all pregnancies in the United States are now
terminated through abortions.

Trying to overturn *Roe vs. Wade* at this juncture,
especially through the proposed Constitutional amendment
process, is akin to trying to restore prohibition or
overturn *Brown vs.The Board of Education* by repealing
the 14th amendment. It's a long and tortuous road that
promises trench warfare in each of 50 state legisla-
tures. Moreover, the impending arrival of RU 486, a
French "morning after" pill that effectively terminates
pregnancies up to nine weeks after conception, buries
the issue deeper since it takes away the gruesome medical imagery that abortion calls up.

And the fact is most Republicans are glad to see it
go away. Exit polls throughout the primary this year
showed a vast majority of Republicans favor a woman's
right to choose. Even more telling, a study of exit
polls in the 1992 presidential election (by Emory
University professor Alan Abramowitz) showed George Bush

lost 17% of the GOP vote because of his party's extreme anti-abortion stance.

"Abortion had a stronger influence on candidate choice than any other policy issue, including affirmative action, social welfare, defense spending, the Gulf War, and the death penalty," Abramowitz concluded.

Dole, too, would like to see this issue go away. But his challenge will be to match up his "Declaration of Tolerance" with a Republican platform that for 12 straight years has asserted "The unborn child has a fundamental individual right to life which cannot be infringed."

As the Republican convention in Texas showed last month, the anti-abortion forces will not go gently into the good night. "When it comes to killing unborn children, there is really no room for tolerance," Bill Price, leader of Texans United for Life, told supporters after capturing 70 of the 90 open seats in the Texas Republican delegation. "This convention has decided to say, 'We're not sending pro-aborts to San Diego to try to change our party platform.'"

"I'm going to San Diego and I'm going to lead this battle to keep our party pro-life," Pat Buchanan told another gathering of Washington State Republicans. "We're going to fight until hell freezes over and then we're going to fight on the ice. You all come down to San Diego and bring your ice skates."

In state conventions in Iowa, Indiana, Maine, Alabama, Virginia, South and North Carolina, Republicans reaffirmed their opposition to any change in the Republican anti-abortion stand. At the same time, Republican governors in New York, California, Illinois, New Jersey, Pennsylvania, Massachusetts, and Connecticut, who want a more "inclusive" abortion plank, are lobbying their delegations to soften the language.

The man in the middle is Republican Platform Committee Chairman Rep. Henry Hyde (R-Ill.), a personal abortion foe and respected chairman of the House Judiciary Committee. Hyde will chair the platform hearings that precede the Republican convention and seek to find a middle ground in well-crafted platform language he can get both sides to sign off on.

Ironically, he need look no further than the Republican's original pronouncement on the issue in 1976. "The question of abortion is one of the most difficult and controversial of our time," the Republicans wrote in their 1976 preamble to the abortion plank. "It is undoubtedly a moral and personal issue, but it also involves complex questions relating to medical science and criminal justice. There are those in our party who favor complete support for the Supreme Court's decision which permits abortion on demand. There are others who share sincere convictions that the Supreme Court's decision must be changed by a constitutional amendment prohibiting all abortions. Others have yet to take a position, or they have assumed a stance somewhere in between polar positions."

Only after scoping the landscape did the
Republicans make their endorsement. "The Republican
Party favors a continuance of the public dialogue on
abortion and supports the efforts of those who seek
enactment of a constitutional amendment to restore pro-
tection of the right to life for unborn children."

It was language Dole could run on for vice president in 1976 and which he would gladly accept in 1996.
If only being a Republican were that simple. **But the
Republican party has been visited in recent years by
a plague of locusts called The Christian Coalition.**

In the Reagan convention of 1980, they succeeded in
truncating the 1976 preamble to a single sentence recog-
nizing "differing views" and, in 1984, eliminating it
altogether for the more strongly worded present version.

Ralph Reed, the executive director of The Christian
Coalition (who was only 12 when *Roe vs. Wade* came down),
has said, "Support for the party among its religious
base will bleed away as if from a slashed artery" if the
current language is watered down.

If Dole wants to galvanize and lead his party forward, he must face down Reed and all the fractious
elements that will surely bring this fight to the floor.
Is the Republican platform position on abortion critical? It's not. It's a platform -- adopted on Monday,
forgotten on Tuesday, and covered over on Wednesday with
bunting and TV cables. What matters in San Diego is not
what the platform says, but what the TV viewers see.
What the viewers want to see is Ol' Fightin' Bob Dole,

standing for change, even if it makes him unpopular with The Right. This is a rare instance where Dole can give them what they want, and be right at the same time.

For Dole to be a credible candidate in the 90's, he must put to rest the issues that divided us in the 70's. There is no going back on *Roe vs. Wade*. No point in disputing a woman's right to choose. Let principled people disagree on their personal choices. It's time to bury this hatchet. For the good of the party. For the good of the nation.

Advisory Board? Count Me In!

Some days being a political correspondent is as easy as falling off a log. The idiots just come to you.

The case in point is the letter that arrived today in the mail from Haley Barbour, Chairman of The Republican National Committee, congratulating me on my nomination to the Chairman's Advisory Board at the Republican Convention in San Diego.

I did not even know I had been nominated until I opened the letter underneath from, of all people, Bob Dole, who also wanted to congratulate me and extend his "personal invitation" to join him on the convention podium.

Bob went on about how much he was looking forward to seeing me in San Diego and even offered me a little inside, professional-to-professional political advice.

"Space inside the San Diego Convention Center is very limited," Bob wrote, "so I have reserved a seat for you because of your outstanding support in the community and for the Republican Party. Please know that this seat cannot be reserved for very long so I need to hear from you as soon as possible."

(YES, BOB, YES! SAVE MY SEAT. I'M THERE FOR YOU. YOU AND ME, ON THE PODIUM, EVERY STEP OF THE WAY. COUNT ME IN! IF IT'S ADVICE YOU WANT, IT'S ADVICE YOU'LL GET. BOB, HEY, BOB. . .)

Well, what with Bob and Haley beating down my door to come to San Diego, I right then picked up the phone and called Bob's man at the Republican National Committee Advisory Board -- Alex Johnson (1-800-762-7764) -- only to learn the cost of accepting the nomination is $5,000, and that's only your check-writer's starter kit.

You also need to cough up $525 per person in event fees, $1,000 for the hotel room, and anywhere from $1,000 to $15,000 -- do you want a seat or a table? -- to attend the coveted Republican Convention Gala on Wednesday night.

The truth is The Republican National Committee Chairman's Advisory Board is one of those "Big Giver" clubs you read about in the *Washington Post* and, given that Clinton's President's Advisory Council charges $50,000 and up (ah, the benefits of incumbency), Bob Dole's promise of two reserved seats at the Republican Convention -- and all the fun you can have in San Diego -- sounded like a real bargain.

A sort of political one-cent sale on clout.

(I'M TELLING YOU, BOB. COUNT THE STUMP IN. I DON'T KNOW HOW I'LL PAY FOR IT. I'LL HAVE A "SEND STUMP TO SAN DIEGO" CONTEST HERE ON THE INTERNET IF I HAVE TO. I'LL SLEEP IN NAVY BUNKS. WEAR POSTER BOARDS IN THE PARKING LOT. BLOW UP BALLOONS. WHATEVER IT TAKES, BOB. MY ADVICE IS YOURS. P.S. CONTEST ENTRANTS: SEND YOUR $5,000 CHECKS TO ME, STUMP @ 1208 WEBSTER, CHICAGO, ILL 60614. IF YOUR CHECK IS CHOSEN FROM THE PILE, YOU CAN WIN A FREE TRIP TO SAN DIEGO WITH STUMP. NO EXPENSES PAID.)

I'm not going to San Diego just because Bob Dole needs some good advice right about now. Judging from Mr. Barbour's four-page invitation, it appears the fate of the nation -- and most of the really good parties -- depend on my participation in The Chairman's Advisory Board.

To garner the affection of those who appreciate really bad direct mail letters, I would like to quote some of the verbiage from Chairman Barbour's invitation.

You can read about these political fat-cat perks in most newspapers, but no one -- except maybe *The Week Behind* -- has the space to let readers see how the bull-shit falls upon the meadow.

Here then is Haley Barbour's explanation of why The Republican Party and, indeed, The Nation, needs Stump's contribution to the Republican Chairman's Advisory Board.

Dear Mr. Connolly:

A few days ago, Senator Bob Dole wrote to inform
you of your nomination to the Chairman's Advisory
Board and to invite you to the 1996 Republican National
Convention from August 11 through August 15.

I am honored to confirm the Senator's invitation, and I
am delighted to extend my personal invitation to you to join
the Chairman's Advisory Board in San Diego, California.

I have enclosed the Chairman's Advisory Board
Convention program information and a membership
acceptance and Convention registration form. Please
review the materials and reply promptly to reserve your
VIP accomodations and Convention credentials.

As Chairman of the Republican Party, I have set
aside a few selected seats for our staunchest party supporters. As a member of the Chairman's Advisory Board,
a seat has been reserved in the Convention Hall for you.
This is particularly important because the facilities
available in San Diego -- while of the very highest quality
-- are simply much smaller than previous Republican
Conventions. It is critical, if you choose to accept this
invitation to join the Chairman's Advisory Board, that
you respond as soon as possible.

At the Convention, you will witness history being
made when Senator Dole and his running mate are for-
mally elected as the 1996 Republican presidential and
vice presidential nominees. You will see firsthand the
beginning of the final stage of the 1996 campaign.

Only once every four years does our Party come together to select its candidate -- and for most people, it's a once-in-a-lifetime experience -- to personally participate in the nomination of the next President of the United States. Not only will 1996 behold the last presidential election of the 20th Century, but it will mark the most important election in political history!

From your reserved seat, you will witness all the proceedings -- from the keynote addresses to the Roll Call of the States to the acceptance speech. At the Convention Center, the Chairman's Advisory Board will also provide a members-only hospitality suite which will give you a chance to meet VIPs in an informal setting.

In addition to Convention sessions, we have also planned a series of exclusive Chairman's Advisory Board off-site events taking advantage of San Diego's premier attractions. During the week, you will hear from elected officials and program participants whose schedules are currently being confirmed. You will also be greeted by Former Vice President and current Honorary Chairman of the Advisory Board, Dan Quayle.

After the morning convention session on Monday, Speaker Newt Gringrich *[sic]* [Advice to Bob #1: Teach The Chairman how to spell The House Speaker's name!] has requested to personally meet with the Chairman's Advisory Board for lunch and a photo opportunity at the old San Diego Yacht Club. That evening, I will be hosting a party at the historic Hotel Del Coronado to salute and thank you and all the members of the Republican

93

National Committee for their hard work.

The next day, Board members will sail aboard the
Lord Hornblower for a luncheon cruise and a tour of San
Diego by water. Following the evening convention ses-
sion, country entertainer Travis Tritt and members of
the Board will honor Speaker Newt Gingrich at a "Great
Country Celebration" under the stars overlooking the
San Diego Bay.

On Wednesday, we will travel up to Yorba Linda,
California, for a lunch and private guided tour of the
Richard Nixon Presidential Library. You will be greeted
and hear from those closest to him. Invited speakers
include Julie Nixon Eisenhower and Tricia Nixon Cox,
the President's two daughters.

On Thursday, the Chairman's Advisory Board members will be treated to a special "Behind the Scenes"
Tour at the World Famous San Diego Zoo. We will be
joined by the 1996 Senate candidates and their families.

The Chairman's Advisory Board is one of the most
active and effective leadership groups within the
national Republican Party. Its executive sessions offer
an exceptional opportunity for you to develop an ongoing
personal acquaintance with the senior leadership of our
Party.

[Friendships are the glue of politics.]

Your decision to join the Chairman's Advisory Board therefore, is probably the most significant step you can take today to help defeat Bill Clinton, reelect a Republican Congress and advance our agenda of lower taxes, a balanced budget, welfare and tort reform and much more . . .

[In fact, there's about six more paragraphs of "more" . . . about labor pouring "tens of millions" into beating Republicans, Clinton "dodging the real issues" and "the news media who voted 12 to 1 for Bill Clinton in 1992, remains overwhelmingly left-liberal in its bias." Right. And the news media who voted 12 to 1 for Bush are right-conservative in their bias.]

Membership in the Chairman's Advisory Board requires an annual contribution of $5,000. One hundred percent of these funds are reserved by the RNC for direct candidate support programs, so a conference fee is also charged attendees to help cover expenses at Board functions.

The Advisory Board meets four times a year with our Party's presidents, presidential candidates, congressional leaders, governors, and other top GOP policy-makers. To foster candid discussion, the Board is selective in character and small enough to permit active personal participation. Your input is sought and your personal counsel is valued.

The friendships you make in San Diego with Republican officeholders and Party officials will be renewed at Chairman's Advisory Board campaign events throughout the year. And next January, your membership will entitle you to VIP accomodations, preferred invitations to all public events, and exclusive Board receptions and briefings as we celebrate President Dole's Inaugural Gala!

Please review the enclosed Chairman's Advisory Board membership acceptance and Convention registration information carefully. I hope you will choose to join us, and I look forward to seeing you in San Diego.

Sincerely,

Haley Barbour
Chairman

P.S. Due to the limited space at the Convention Center, please return your membership acceptance and Convention registration materials as soon as possible. If you have further questions about your Chairman's Advisory Board membership or arrangements for the Convention, please feel free to call the Board's membership director, Alex Johnson, at (800) 762-7764 or (202) 863-8679. Thank you.

ALEX, BOOK THE PLANE. I'M THERE. SEE YOU ON THE TARMAC.

Armchair Quarterback

Well, I guess it should have been obvious the "Send Stump to San Diego" contest was not going to turn out as well as I hoped.

That little snafu in the platform committee on abortion? I would never have advised that. But then, **I AM NOT** on Bob Dole's Advisory Board to The Republican Convention. Am I?

I did not get to go on board the *Lord Hornblower* cruise of the San Diego Bay. I did not have Julie Nixon Eisenhower's personal tour of the Nixon library in Yorba Linda. **I DID NOT EVEN GET INVITED** to Dan Quayle's Charity Golf Tournament -- that charity being the Republican Party -- for $75,000 a pop.

Noooooooooo..wo..wo..wo wo wo... my seat went to some wealthier advisor who could afford the $5,000 fee.

Well, screw you Bob. Let him get you out of this mess.

I myself have bigger fish to fry this weekend... because right after I clarified my role on the board with Chairman Haley's man over at Republican HQ, I got a call from The Old Speaker of The House Himself -- Mr. Newtster to you -- asking whether he might stop by in Chicago for a little **FREE ADVICE** on his way out to chair the convention.

Now, I don't know about you, but I live in a respectable neighborhood. We barbeque on the front stoop, blow off fire hydrant caps in the summer, and talk among ourselves a lot.

"I can't be bringing you down my block," I told Newt. "What will the neighbors say? How about we find someplace neutral. Someplace where you won't stand out so much," I said.

"Is it the color of my skin? Is it because I'm white?" he asked.

"It's the clothes, Newt. You have to wear something less geeky."

"I'll tell you what. I have just the place," Newt said. "Let's meet in Dixon, Ronald Reagan's old hometown. It's only two hours out of Chicago. I'll get us some rooms at the Presidential Inn... and I'll work on the clothes."

I had to pause for a minute, wondering whether I was able to give The Republicans one more piece of advice, one more time. Oh hell, I decided, I'll do it on spec.

"Okay, I'll meet you in Dixon," I told him. "But I'm bringing my camera. When you go out there and electrify the convention next week, I want people to know where you got the bright idea."

"I'll tell them from Ronald Reagan," he laughed. "See you there."

I did indeed go to Dixon last weekend and stayed in The Presidential Inn. That car you see in the picture is my '74 Pontiac and the black van in the corner is the vehicle the Secret Service brought along.

Newt took me to dinner at The White House.

We sat under a glass case filled with old handguns, ate fried chicken, and talked about whether the Sox can catch Cleveland if Frank Thomas doesn't come back full-strength. Newt's an okay guy if you get him on the subject of baseball. But he doesn't know beans. He just sort of nods like he does.

The next morning we got up early and started the advising. We talked farm policy.

99

<u>visited a missile site</u> and, of course, paid our respects at the <u>Boyhood Home of Ronald Reagan.</u>

By the end of the day, I felt pretty confident I was getting through to Newt. Whatever happens, I said, stay out of the line of fire.

<u>What you have to do out there</u> is be firm but compassionate. Your best ten minutes are going to be your first ten minutes. Monday night. After the networks pick you up. Around 9 or 10 PM Eastern. That's when you set the whole pace and tone. That's when you become you.

Don't worry about what C-SPAN and CNN are doing up to then. They'll pick you up around 3 PM and stay with every boring minute. Use the afternoon to practice your quick roll calls. The money shot is when the networks come on. Treat the networks right and they'll treat you right. What you really want to do here, mediawise, is CONTROL PRIMETIME. Make it your own. Make that convention run like clockwork. Steamroller that thing if you have to. It doesn't matter what anybody says on the abortion plank -- as long as they say it quickly.

If you can just make sure the train runs on time, get everybody in and out of there on cue and run an efficient convention, who knows, people might start believing you can run the government.

The key to Monday night is to **get into the show flow** right off the bat. See it from the man in the control booth's point of view: A succession of mean-ingless events that must be packaged together tightly into primetime entertainment as if something important is happening -- even though it is not.

Ideally, you'd like them to cut to you around 9:08 or 9:10 PM. You don't want to step on the anchors when they're doing their "Here I am again on the convention floor." But you also don't want to give them too much time or they'll find some kookie delegate who's got a problem with his seat; and before you know it, you got a demonstration going.

Keep some marching bands and local secretaries of state in back in case you need them. If you get a demon-stration you don't want -- be careful, there are some demonstrations you want -- send the marching band over in front of the camera platform. And in the afternoons, when you're using up all these speakers on debates no one wants to hear, stuff the secretaries of state in-between to pad out the time so your main event doesn't start too early.

Ah yes, The Main Event. You're not it. Your job is to get 'em on and get 'em off -- and glad-hand them on the way up and down. And whatever you do, don't say anything controversial. You want to trumpet up American values, pick something everyone can believe in -- like beach volleyball.

If everything goes well, Bob Dole's going to get the credit. If everything goes badly, make sure you don't take the fall.

And when Dole comes on Thursday to claim the nomination, **get the hell out of the picture.** Don't leave any evidence you were there.

I thought Newt took my advice well. I waved good-bye to my new best friend certain that he'd come back -- if not soon, in four years. I can't say it's all going to come down just

like we planned it, but don't blame me. I'm off the Bob Dole advisory board. My man is Newt, and from here on in, as far as I can see, it's all a matter of execution.

Listen My Children

My children tell me the Sixties nostalgia craze is over. My vinyls of Jimi Hendrix have returned to their original value, Nehru jackets are not in style, and the big news these days is the comeback tour of Metallica.

In the car on the way to tennis camp, my eleven-year-old tried to explain to me how we lost Vietnam because we weren't allowed to win it. (My seven-year-old thinks its because our bombs weren't big enough.) And it occurred to me that it might be time to pull them on my knee and tell them of a time when the truth did make us free.

The year was 1968. America had been fighting the war in Vietnam, by virtue of a Congressional resolution, for four years. Our commitment of ground troops to the venture had reached 466,000 soldiers and 20,000 of them had already died.

In January, the Viet Cong launched a Tet Offensive that, as Peter Arnett described it, "rolled across Saigon like a tidal wave over a landfill."

In February, General Westmoreland requested 200,000 more troops, and a little-known Minnesota senator named Eugene McCarthy challenged President Johnson in the March 12th New Hampshire primary to reverse America's commitment to "win" the war.

Busloads of "Clean for Gene" college students, fearful of campus demonstrations where cohorts calling themselves "The Resistance" burned draft cards, poured into the state to "work within the system." For the first time in America's history, McCarthy beat a sitting president in a Democratic primary by opposing a war we were on the wrong side of.

Four days later, Bobby Kennedy announced he too would run against President Johnson.

On March 31st, President Johnson, now the embodiment of "The War," pulled a Bob Dole. He went before the nation, three days before the Wisconsin primary, and declared he would not be a candidate for re-election, but would stake his reputation on his ability to bring "Peace in Vietnam." Hubert Humphrey, his vice president, would run in his stead.

On April 4th, a crazed gunman, James Earl Ray, shot Martin Luther King on a motel balcony in Memphis. Instantaneously, fires were kindled in the inner cities of Memphis, Harlem, Brooklyn, Detroit, Washington,

Newark, Boston, and Chicago. On April 23rd, students at Columbia University barricaded themselves in the dean's office in an antiwar protest.

On May 10th, like a wave rippling across the Atlantic, French students rioted through the streets of Paris and nearly toppled the regime of Charles DeGaulle; Czechoslovakian students, living in Prague under the democratic reforms of Prime Minister Dubcek, also braced themselves for an invasion by 400,000 Russian troops.

On June 4th, Bobby Kennedy stunned Humphrey with a victory in the California primary. **"I want to thank you all for your support. . . Now it's on to Chicago and victory,"** Bobby told a ballroom crowd in Los Angeles. The next day, he was dead.

In July, an obscure Senator from South Dakota, George McGovern, picked up the Kennedy mantle and threw his hat in the ring, and two self-promoting antiwar hippies, Abbie Hoffman and Jerry Rubin, calling themselves the Youth International or Yippie Party, invited the youth of America to a "Festival of Life" during the 1968 Democratic convention in Chicago -- which took place that August.

"A Constitutional Convention is being planned," Hoffman wrote in the *Realist*, his political magazine. "Visionary mind-benders who will for five long days and nights address themselves to the task of formulating the goals and means of the New Society. It will be a blend of technologists and poets, of artists and community organizers, of anyone who has a vision. We will try to develop a Community of Consciousness.

"There will be a huge rock-folk festival for free," he continued. **"Workshops in a variety of subjects such as draft resistance, drugs, commune development, guerilla theater and underground media.** There will probably be a huge march across town to haunt the Democrats. People coming to Chicago should begin preparations for five days of energy-exchange. Do not come prepared to sit down and watch and be fed and cared for."

I arrived by train on a sunny Sunday afternoon after a summer of pushing bull ladles in a foundry in Milwaukee. I was 18.

The concourse of Union Station was filled with McCarthy recruiters, prowling the platforms looking for people to help run the mimeograph machines and promising a room, at the Wabash YMCA for $11 a night, to anyone who signed on.

They took me to the Y in a Volkswagen van covered in McCarthy daisy stickers and those craw-footed peace symbols.

It was right smack downtown, overlooking the parking lot of the Hilton Hotel, where Johnson and Humphrey (and most of the working press) were encamped.

I walked over to the Hilton. The turmoil soon to become known as the "Convention Riots" could be smelled in the acid air. Someone had blown off a stink bomb in the hotel air-conditioning system and it lingered in every rancid corner of the hotel. The smell would last all week, worsening every day, a sign of things to come.

I walked to the other headquarter's hotels and found in each someone I knew, squirreled away in a corner, running press releases to the media, folding T-shirts into delegate bags, or otherwise doing their part to stop the war.

Sunday night, hoping to catch the Festival of Life before the 11 PM curfew, I hailed a cab to go to Lincoln Park. The driver would go no closer than the exit ramp on Lake Shore Drive so I hoofed it, following the sound of bongo drums, through a back parking lot to the lighted bonfires in the distance. Yes, the smell of marijuana was in the air.

The parking lot was sealed off by rows of school busses filled with Chicago police. I searched for a breach in the line, walking up and down the length of busses. The police banged their nightsticks and riot helmets on the windows daring me to cross.

At curfew time, the festival goers in the park were down to six or seven hundred, but thousands of onlookers (and media) lined the sidewalks curious to see the outcome. Police cars wove through the park announcing the park closing, and some students piled benches into a makeshift barricade. Suddenly, over the rise, an armored vehicle appeared with hundreds of police marching along in sweeping lines. Tear gas bombs streamed overhead. People broke for the streets in panic. The police gave chase and waded into the crowd, billy clubs flailing. The war was coming home.

On Monday, the news of the Lincoln Park riot circu-
lated slowly among the delegates breakfasting in the
Hilton. (The heavy rioting had taken place after midnight and news reports appeared only in the re-plated
late city editions.) There was a good amount of talk,
particularly among the reporters, about the large number
of reporters beaten in the melee. **But the more
(de)pressing news was that the joker who set off the
stink bomb in the Hilton had done it again; just as
Hubert Humphrey was arriving to claim his nomination.**

I joined Hoffman, Rubin, Tom Hayden, the leader of
Students for a Democratic Society, and David Dellinger,
a peace activist who had organized The March on The
Pentagon the year before, in a march to the old Chicago
Coliseum for an "anti-birthday" party for LBJ. Phil Ochs
sang a verse of "It's always the old who lead us to war;
it's always the young who fall," and the crowd responded
with raised fists and a chant, "Hell no, we won't go."

In Lincoln Park again that night, joined by 400
clergymen carrying a huge wooden cross, the protestors
prepared to defend their turf in a non-violent vigil.
Allen Ginsberg, Jean Genet, William Burroughs, and Terry
Southern -- on assignment from *Esquire* magazine -- sat
in the middle, Ginsberg chanting "OM" and tinkling his
little finger cymbals.

"It happened all in an instant," Steve Lerner wrote
in the Village Voice. *"The night which had been filled
with darkness and whispers exploded in a fiery scream.
Huge tear-gas canisters came crashing through the*

branches, snapping them, and bursting in the center of the gathering. From where I lay, groveling in the grass, I could see ministers retreating with the cross, carrying it like a fallen comrade. Another volley shook me to my feet. Gas was everywhere. People were running, screaming, tearing through the trees.

"The police were advancing in a picket line, swatting at the stragglers and crumpled figures; huge trucks, usually used for cleaning the streets, swept toward us spraying more gas. Kids began ripping up the pavement and hurling snowball-size chunks at the truck windows. Then they flooded out into the streets, blocking traffic, fighting with plainclothesmen who awaited our exodus from the park, and bombarding hapless patrol cars, which sped through the crowds."

"I flashed First World War doughboys caught in no-man's-land during a mustard gas attack. I felt sure I was going to die. I heard others choking around me. And then everything cleared," Lerner reported.

By Tuesday night,the proceedings inside the convention hall were beginning to reflect the chaos on the streets. CBS newsman Mike Wallace was punched and dragged from the floor defending the credentials of a New York delegate. McCarthy and McGovern forces tried to raise the street violence as an issue, but were gaveled out of order.

In the early hours of Wednesday morning, after being evicted from Lincoln Park, the protestors regrouped across the street from the Hilton in Grant Park. There were now thousands, not hundreds.

At two, three, and four in the morning, as the convention delegates straggled back to their rooms, they
could smell the tear gas and hear the defiant chants.

*"All night they could hear the demonstrators chant-
ing, ' join us, join us' and the college below of utter
contempt, 'Dump the Hump! Dump The Hump!'"* Norman Mailer
wrote in Miami and The Siege of Chicago. *"All the fury of
the beatings and the tear-gassings, all the bitter disap-
pointments of the recently elapsed bright spring when the
only critical problem was who would make a better
President, Kennedy or McCarthy (now all the dread of a
future with Humphrey or Nixon.) There was the sense that
police had now entered their lives, become an element per-
vasive as drugs and books and sex and music and family. So
they shouted up to the windows of the Hilton. . . they
called up through the night on a stage as vast and tower-
ing as one of Wagner's visions and the screams of police
cars joined them, pulling up, gliding away, blue lights
revolving, lines of police hundreds long in their sky-blue
shirts and sky-blue crash helmets, penning the demonstrators back of barriers across Michigan Avenue from the
Hilton and other lines of police and police fences on the
Hilton's side of the street."*

On Wednesday afternoon, while Humphrey polished
his acceptance speech in the Hilton, a final antiwar
rally -- to be followed by an "illegal" march to the
convention hall -- was called for 1 PM in Grant Park.
As "the kids" gathered one more time, a funny thing
started happening. Office workers in the Loop slipped
over to the park to join them. Delegates left their

hotels and wandered over. The crowd was ten times that of the previous night.

The speeches were just getting underway when three boys attempted to pull down an American flag and a squad of police waded into the crowd to stop them. The police unleashed their tear gas canisters, and the demonstrators tossed them back. More police charged into the crowd and Tom Hayden, one of the last to appear on the podium before chaos erupted, urged the assembled crowd to break into small groups "to do what you have to do." **The Battle of Michigan Avenue was joined.**

On the television sets of America, the convention session that night, with its cries of "Gestapo tactics on the streets of Chicago," was punctuated by 17 minutes of footage shot under glaring lights from platform trucks outside on Michigan Avenue and raced to the networks for instant air. (This was before CNN, in the pre-minicam days when mobile cameras only shot film, which had to be processed and developed before broadcast.) It was a controversial, but by no means exaggerated view of a most unusual time.

You will see these pictures a lot in the coming month as the Democrats gather in Chicago this August. **I'm in there someplace. So are most of your parents.**

When I hear Bob Dole talk about battling for the "heart and soul" of the Republican party in San Diego, it's a faint echo of what took place during the Democratic convention of 1968. It was the heart and soul of the nation that came apart that year and the pieces fell to those demonstrators on the streets of Chicago to pick up and put back together over the next 25 years.

In *The New Yorker* this week, Richard Nixon's assistant, Monica Crowley, recalls sitting with Nixon in 1992 listening to a news report on Bill Clinton's efforts to avoid the draft. "I know why he did what he did to dodge the draft; he didn't want to get his ass shot off," Nixon said. "As I was out there, trying to end the God-damned war, he was running around claiming privilege, avoiding service, and demonstrating against it."

In Nixon's voice I can hear my father's. The generational conflict was always there. And it was not all that easy being on our side of the gap.

You always knew and feared people would see your protests as draft-dodging, self-interest, or cowardice. As much as we told ourselves the greatest patriots are those who tell the country when it's wrong, few believed it and fewer still thought patriotism came in 18-year-old packages.

What the Chicago Convention Riots provided was a moment of truth for our generation, when the time came to act on our principles and rise above our fear and confusion to show what, in war, is sometimes called courage.

And when we did, we found our hearts and souls weren't in a party, or even in the nation, but in ourselves -- and each other. **What the '68 Convention taught us was that a little bit of anarchy is all right, and might be good for the country.**

Six years and 35,000 American deaths later, the War in Vietnam, doomed from the beginning, ended with the fall of Saigon in 1974.

Jerry Rubin became a health-food guru, stockbroker, and investment counsellor who died, at the age of 56, when he was hit by a car crossing Wilshire Boulevard in Hollywood.

Abbie Hoffman was busted for cocaine, went underground and became an environmental activist for 13 years before he died of a barbituate overdose at the age of 52.

Tom Hayden,56, now a California state senator representing Beverly Hills, will be back this year as a delegate to the '96 Convention.

David Dellinger,81, has applied for a permit to conduct a protest demonstration in Grant Park.

Before he died, Hoffman returned to Chicago for a symposium held on the 20th anniversary of the '68 Convention. He took the podium with the same impish grin that started it all.

"We were young," he told the crowd. "We were impetuous. We were arrogant. . . and we were right."

All power to the people.

At The End Of The Day

At the end of the day, Republican National Chairman Haley Barbour was telling Pat Robertson on my favorite convention TV show -- the *700 Club* -- on the Christian Broadcasting Network. . . .

All The Republicans really wanted to do in San Diego was to equalize the numbers.

"They (The Democrats) have been squealing like stuck pigs (about) their lead in the polls," Barbour, the Texas-drawling Republican, told Robertson, the former presidential candidate (1988) and majority owner (can anyone here say Gene Autry?) of the 44-million-subscriber Christian Broadcasting Network.

"My goal, and I've always said this, was to come out of the convention in a two-way race, with Dole hanging around 42% or 43%, which is really just keeping our base intact," Barbour said.

"Are the Democrats going to get a bump when their convention comes around? Sure, but what I'm hoping is that, at the end of the day, we're in a 50-50 race after Labor Day."

"At the end of the day" is one of Stump's favorite expressions in politics. It means, in consultant par-lance, "Okay, so my guy goofed up. Your guy is gonna goof up and, if we position the positives right and counter-balance our negatives, when we get to the real mud-slinging . . . at the end of the day. . . we'll be right in there."

John Buckley, the Dole campaign communications director, said it best Sunday at the beginning of con-vention week. "There's nothing wrong with our campaign that a good running mate, a good convention, and $60 million in advertising can't fix." And a lot of people will come out of this week believing they've done it.

The game in San Diego was poll numbers

-- staying on message, bridging the gender gap, shunning controversy, appearing inclusive, grabbing "The Big Mo" and putting on a good show.

It was a show designed and orchestrated by Paul Manafort and Michael Deaver, the Washington political con-sultants whose last big makeover project was Ronald Reagan.

I thought I ought to watch the whole convention -- as a professional courtesy -- gavel to gavel, Monday thru Thursday, 5-10 PM -- just to be in the swim at the water cooler. But it was an impossible task, not only because nothing was actually worth watching, but because even when you watched The Republican Convention, you weren't sure what you were seeing.

Imagine being trapped in a room, forced to watch a Solaflex infomercial 40 times, then being asked your opinion of the actor's muscle tone in Part IV - Bicept Restoral.

No wonder Ted Koppel pulled out after Day Two. We political commentators have our dignity, as slight as it is.

The way to watch The Republican Convention last week was not to watch it at all. Turn on the car radio in a traffic jam to NPR, catch the sound bites on *The Morning News* when you're half-asleep, let the TV play in the background during dinner and read a newspaper every once in a while. The Republican Party nominated Bob Dole for president last week. Are you surprised?

I like the way everyone I know, none of whom actually paid attention to the convention, had an opinion about it. If they didn't actually see some event, they'd seen some filtered version of it, or sound bite from it, or comment on the sound bite that formed their opinion of it.

If something didn't happen on the TV channel you were watching, you could assume it happened because things like that always happen during conventions. And if you have better things to do in August than watch nothing happen on TV, you're grateful for all the spin the commentators have put on things.

116

When the office gathers around the water cooler in the morning, whatever filtered version of the filtered version of reality you have, like bottled water poured through a sieve, is somehow safer because it reflects someone else's opinion.

"What'd ya think of Jack Kemp? Great choice, huh?" Bryen, the sound guy, said when I walked into the kitchen Monday morning after Dole announced his VP pick.

"Good quarterback, but he never won a Superbowl," I said.

"Did they have Superbowls back then?" Bryen asked.

"I rest my case," I said.

"Looks like Kemp is going to give Dole a real advantage," C.C. Creams, our video editor and erstwhile junior political correspondent, announced to me Tuesday morning. "The ABC/CNN tracking poll is showing a one point bump today."

"Give it time," I said. "It'll be 10 by Friday. They haven't even gotten to women's day yet."

On Wednesday, women who wouldn't know Harry Truman from Harry Houdini were asking, "What do you think of Susan Molinari?"

"Barbie in a business suit," Creams sniffed.

"I thought she was really a powerful speaker, very perky. She really responded well to the camera and made a good case for all of us," one of the women in the office said.

"She really let Clinton have it, didn't she?" said another.

"People I talk to say she's a real force in the party," said a third.

"Oh yeah? What do you know about her?" I asked. "What borough in New York does she represent? What office does she hold? How long has she been there? What has she ever done?"

It did not surprise me Wednesday morning when the ABC/CNN Wednesday tracking poll had the race at a ten-point spread, Clinton 47 - Dole 37, with Ross Perot picking up 12%. The woman's vote -- so anti-Dole up to now -- was clearly softening.

"Doesn't it bother you that you, a woman, are responding to an event scripted by the most cynical political operative in Washington, a man, who reviews every speech, writes every sound bite, edits every video clip, and calls every camera shot?" I asked.

"But that baby was so cute. It looks just like her," she said.

Thursday morning, people thought I should be impressed Elizabeth Dole could walk around the convention floor like Oprah for 20 minutes without a teleprompter. "Stunning," they said on CBS. "A star turn," ABC reported. "It will be hard for Bob Dole to top his wife," a PBS commentator intoned.

Well, Stump here admires Liddie Dole's performance
as much as the next guy, but isn't Wednesday night the
time they call the roll and choose the candidate? Did I
miss something on the networks? Or did Manafort and
Deaver just decide to pass up this detail because of a
scheduling conflict with Letterman and Leno?

Allow me to digress. I was watching *Entertainment
Tonight* and they reported that the networks, who have
already reduced their coverage to an hour of primetime a
night, are thinking of passing on the next convention in
2000, and leaving it to the cable channels.

The combined ratings of ABC, NBC, and CBS for their convention coverage this week has been abysmal -- 12% of the TV-watching public. In 1992, the combined ratings were 16%. By comparison, ABC alone drew a 20% audience share Tuesday night showing a rerun of *The Amy Fisher Story.*

There's little doubt the Republican convention
organizers took a few hints from the NBC Olympics this
year. Timeshift events, blackout contests you don't want
the public to see, and present a "scripted" version of
the day the way the public "wants" to see it unfold.

I say, if we're in for a penny, why not in for a
pound? How about next time, The Republican Party sells
off the exclusive TV rights to their convention to CNN
or MSNBC for, say, $20 million and gets a free web site
out of the deal.

Stop soaking cities for the right to hold the convention, and start soaking the media. Stop trying to manipulate the media, and just give the whole business of politics over to it. Let's privatize political conventions!

Let some media conglomerate run the whole shebang, use their expertise to make the public watch, get better control of the T-shirt and lunchbox concessions, and make a profit off this thing.

Instead of genuflecting in front of the 16,000 mooches who call themselves media representatives, make 'em jealous, give them a TV guide and a channel clicker, and tell them to get their own motel reservations.

We could sell sponsorships for the main events. . . Bill Clinton's acceptance speech brought to you by Arch Deluxe. . . Bob Dole, another fine Sominex product . . . and the party wouldn't have to put all that money into touchy-feely, videowall presentations that no one carries. The sponsoring network would do it for them.

If we really want to do it right, we'll let John Tesh write the music.

And, hey, if this thing catches on, we can solve the whole campaign finance reform problem by selling candidate sponsorships in the primaries:

Baldwin Piano presents Lamar Alexander. . . Air Buchanan -- "Just Nuke It"

-- sponsored by Nike. . . Steve Forbes, a paid political advertisement from *Forbes* magazine. . . But I digress.

Thursday morning's tracking poll results were not encouraging. As highly as the commentators rated Liddie Dole's performance. The ABC/CNN tracking polls showed no change in Dole's approval rating.

"No Bounce," Politicsnow.com headlined. Dole's deficit to Clinton, having narrowed ten points in two days, actually rose from 10% to 11% Thursday morning. The last best hope would be Bob Dole's acceptance speech Thursday night.

"Bob Dole, the most optimistic man in America, trying to turn the corner in the most important speech of his life," as Ted Koppel put it on *Nightline*, capturing in one phrase a 55-minute oration Dole delivered to, in a best case, what might have been 12% of the American public.

(Ironic, huh, how only 24 hours after swearing off the convention as an "infomercial," Koppel was back "at the end of the day" to discuss the Republicans' chances of pulling off a Dole victory in November.)

The highlight of *Nightline* was a secret group of 36 fence-sitting Republicans, Democrats, and Independents ABC had assembled in San Diego, with the help of

Republican political consultant Dan Lundin, to watch every speech and press a red, white, or blue buzzer to indicate their palm sweat reaction.

Here was a media breakthrough. While we watched the videos of Bailey Kay Hutchinson, Susan Molinari, John McClain, and Elizabeth Dole, we could also watch a tracking graph showing the moment-to-moment palm-sweat responses of the focus group, sequestered in a motel room, pressing buttons during each and every moment of each and every speech.

If you think "tracking polls" are specious, with their daily reliance on telephone pollsters to contact and solicit the opinion of 1,000 randomly-selected voters on events that (a) transpired less than an hour before, and (b) may or may not have been seen by the respondees, **consider the statistical accuracy of ABC's Focus Group -- 36 mildly-committed voters, equally split among their expressed party preferences, willing to forgo a week in August to watch nothing happen.**

There's no doubt the novelty of seeing a voter group respond to a speech on TV, in comparable windows on our screen, was visually remarkable and scientifically cool. Except. . . it's a trick. It's a gimmick.

I think the fact people's palm sweat went up over Colin Powell, didn't tic the meter on women's day, and zoomed through the roof when Elizabeth Dole delivered her valentine to Bob is worth contemplating. I believe everything I see on TV.

But statistically, if one of the 12 Republicans in this ABC Focus Group pressed the wrong button at the wrong time, Liddie Dole's ratings would have looked like George Cooney's sliding a scalpel into the wrong heart on ER. I guess what Ted Koppel taught us this year, as keeper of our journalistic ethics, is make sure your opinion is right, because your methodology stinks.

At the end of the day -- and moments after I publish this commentary -- the ABC/CNN tracking poll will report the combined results of asking 1,037 registered voters over the two days of Thursday and Friday, August 15th and 16th, who they will support for president.

My guess -- The Stump Line -- is the results will be Clinton 44, Dole 40, Perot 12.

But the beauty and problem with polling at the end of the day is that no one can second guess you. And another day begins tomorrow.

What Trees Do They Plant?

The Weeping Willow of Peace was Tom Hayden's suggestion for burying the hatchet on the '68 convention riots, and it was the subject of many hearty "belly laughs," according to Chicago *Sun-Times* columnist Michael Sneed, when Hayden, now 56, met with Richard M. Daley, 54, in The Mayor's City Hall office last June.

Hayden, now a California state senator from Beverly Hills, wanted a "healing" rally in the Arie Crown Theater followed by a ceremonial tree-planting in the park. To which the mayor allegedly responded, "But the tree has to survive. We have to water it."

It is my civic shame to have to report "The Weeping Willow of Peace" will not be planted in Grant Park this week during the Democratic Convention.

"We are gonna rock and roll from noon to 3 PM, and then plant the tree at 4 PM," a jubilant Stephanie Rubin, Hayden's spokeswoman, told Sneed, "but we are still trying to figure out if we can plant that kind of tree."

Michael Butler, the Chicago millionaire who produced the 60's musical, *Hair,* would donate the weeping willow and, for a moment, it looked to Stump like Daley had come up with yet another masterstroke of made-for-TV pablum.

What a photo opportunity! With Chicago glistening in the background -- a Chicago Daley has just spent $49 million in public funds beautifying - the new mayor walks across the old '68 battleground, arm in arm with his father's arch foe, leading an Abraham Lincoln Brigade of old hippies carrying shovels to officially declare the Vietnam War over.

And when they stop, they will be standing in front of the Congress and Balbo bridges -- the centerpoint of the Grant Park riots -- where the new Mayor Daley has just poured $16 million into monument cleaning, sculpture gardens, and ornamental light poles that Blair Kamin, architectural critic of the *Chicago Tribune,* describes as "a picture of normalcy, a perfect place for TV reporters to do their standups."

That sly dog Daley, I thought, he'll bury the hatchet all right. Right in Hayden's forehead. This will show 'em what you can do if you just stay home and take over the family business.

"It's Over," Sneed reported two days later in the *Sunday Sun-Times*. The Chicago Park District has sent Hayden a letter stating the tree planting is off because willow trees don't grow if you plant them in August.

I immediately called one of the mayor's political consultants. "You're making a big mistake here," I said.

"Trees don't grow in August," he said. "The Mayor likes his trees. He doesn't want to plant a tree that's going to die."

"But the belly laugh? The watering joke? How did Sneed get the story so wrong?" I asked.

"She forgot to call me," he said.

I called another friend, a Defender of The Mayor, who knows a little about horticulture herself.

A Defender of The Mayor is an old Chicago newspaper term left over from that time when the late Mayor Daley's press secretary told reporters to "write what the mayor means, not what he says." Since Mayor Daley Sr. never actually talked to reporters, the way around the problem was to find someone The Mayor did talk to, who would then convey the gist of his thinking, which was then attributed to A Defender of The Mayor.

"Are you going to see The Mayor, Jr. any time soon?" I asked, "I think he's missing a great opportunity on this tree planting."

"Forget it. Nobody can tell The Mayor anything about trees," The Defender of The Mayor said. "He fancies himself an expert. I was with him at a dinner party once and he was going on and on about these red maples on the South Side he wanted planted all over the city. Well, red maples are a very hard tree to grow outside of certain areas, but he wouldn't hear it. When The Mayor likes a tree, he loves a tree. Planting trees is his thing. Like golf for presidents."

"That's why he should do the ceremony. It's perfect," I said.

"But you don't plant trees in August," she said. "Everyone knows that."

"There's got to be a tree you can plant in August," I said. "He's planted 500,000 trees in Chicago since 1990. What do all the tree planters do in August, take summer vacation?"

"If you can find a tree, I'm sure he'd be happy to plant it. Here's the number of the Chicago Botanical Gardens tree and shrub hotline. Give them a call," she said. So now we were getting somewhere.

Having just been enlisted into The Mayor's service, I went down to the water cooler for a cup of java and ran into Herb, the voiceover guy.

"How about a Passion Flower?" he said. "My wife just bought one. It's a perfect tree for a politician -- it's a climber and a grabber. You bury it about two feet deep in the soil, then when it climbs out, it grabs onto anything that's nearby. We planted ours yesterday."

"How about a Passion Flower?" I asked the mayor's defender.

"There's the problem in a nutshell," she said. "The Passion Flower only blooms once, then it dies in December."

"But that's after the election," I said. "No one is going to know."

"I think that defeats the purpose," she said.

I called The Botanical Gardens Hotline.

"I'm thinking of planting a willow tree this August. Is there any one you'd recommend?" I asked.

"Whatever you do, don't get a corkscrew willow," the volunteer on the other end of the line told me. "I had one in my yard. It sheds leaves all over the place. It finally was struck by lightning a couple years ago and I never replaced it."

"We don't want a tree that's going to be struck by lightning. How about a weeping willow?" I asked.

"You need a lot of room for a willow. They have massive roots."

"Oh, we got plenty of room. We just need something we can plant next week as kind of a peace memorial."

"Stay away from a weeping willow. They're really hard to mow the lawn under."

She thumbed through an index of willow species. "Here's something you might try. The white willow, *salix alba*, grows in zones two to eight, needs wet places and full sun, and it's easily transplanted. . . it's also an upright willow so the grass will grow better."

"And it can be planted in August?" I asked.

"It's better to plant in September or October, but sometimes you just have to plant trees when you plant them."

I thanked her profusely for her help.

"It also says here you can plant a pussy willow," she said.

"I don't think that's the image we're going for," I said.

I called back the Defender of The Mayor with our options. "Look, it's not ideal, but let's face it, we're just planting a metaphor. If it dies in a couple years, who's going to know?" I said.

"You don't get it. The mayor thinks we're planting a tree. A real tree. He just spent $16 million fixing up Grant Park and he's not going to have some dead willow muck it up when everyone's come and gone."

"That's the same problem we had with his father," I said. "Okay, I have one last suggestion. The Contorted Filbert. It's small. It doesn't take up much space. It only grows two inches a year. It will be 30 years before anyone realizes it's dead."

The Defender thought about it. "A Contorted Filbert might work. But you haven't gotten around the main problem. It's not planting season."

Last Sunday I picked up the *New York Times* and there, on page 16, was a picture of a Chicago city worker hauling two behemoth trees out of a fork lift. "Chicago Spruces Up For Return Of Party," said the headline.

I called my friend, the Mayor's Defender, to see what gives. **"Let me put it this way," she said. "The mayor doesn't want to do it. So it's not going to happen."**

"Oh," I said, "now that's another story."

Sneaking In!

Editor's Note: So many parties, so little time. Stump's Democratic Convention coverage begins today. More convention reports will appear throughout the week if anything happens.

I learned this lesson early in life. No one ever invites you to join a political party. You have to sneak in.

That dictum is never more true than during a political convention. The Democrats, for instance, rented the United Center (capacity 22,000) and promptly closed off two-thirds of it to make a TV studio for the 4,320 delegates who attended.

It was four days of television you could ignore, and if you didn't get enough of it, you are a glutton for punishment.

As a member of the media, I, of course, could have picked up my press credentials any time. But the action last week was not in the convention hall. It was on the party circuit.

With the assistance of my faithful companion, *Plus One*, I set out to cover the story behind the story, the parties behind the party, keeping in mind **Stump's Law: I never met a convention I couldn't break into.**

It was a tough agenda -- a non-stop grind of work, work, work that started with an Aretha Franklin concert in Grant Park Friday night and didn't end until The President joined me for an intimate dinner in the Sheraton Ballroom after his acceptance speech Thursday night.

We had boat rides and art museums and hip clubs to go to; celebrity Democrats to run into; fans to fend off; and fun to burn. . . 4,200 officially-sanctioned parties in four days...but I'm getting ahead of myself...again.

SUNDAY -- A DAY TO REMEMBER

Just to make sure nobody double-crossed nobody -- as we say in Chicago -- I went down to the Arie Crown Theater Sunday afternoon to see that Tom Hayden didn't go planting any trees on the sneak.

It was an odd scene, a cavernous auditorium only half filled with people, most of whom were well up in their years. I shelled out $10 for Hayden's new book, *The Whole World Was Watching*, with all proceeds going to something called The Guacamole Fund. "It's Tom's think tank thing," the salesman said. When Hayden announced later the rally was produced courtesy of Avocado Productions, I started to worry. Has Hayden gone veggie on us?

132

The media prowled the hallways looking for recogniz-
able faces. I saw John Froines, one of the original Chicago
7 defendants, in grey hair and a professorial sweater-vest
talking to a news crew from *Iowa TV Tonight* and E.J.
Dionne, the twerpy *Washington Post* columnist, telling a
French TV crew in French "l'administration du Clinton avec
nous May-yor Day-lee" has the situation well under control.

If you were old, smiling, and wearing a Grateful
Dead T-shirt, you could get a camera stuck in your face
and talk for hours.

"Who's that?" I asked a reporter watching a couple
of 22-year old youths with a DVC camcorder work over
some guy in the corner.

"That's Stew Albert."

"Who's he?" I asked.

"I don't know. Some old hippie who tells a good
story," he said.

Inside the hall, a lone peace symbol was projected
through the darkness onto a wall. Norman Mailer read moving excerpts from his 1968 remembrance of Bobby Kennedy's
funeral; Bonnie Raitt played protest songs with Stephen
Stills and Graham Nash; Jackson Brown made his customary
appearance. Bella Abzug lit the fire of womanhood, and
Jesse Jackson -- watch out for that Jesse! -- found his
metier recalling and reviving the spirit of '68.

Outside, the ubiqitous Bill Stamets, documentarian
of all things political, and his photographer friend

from the *LA Weekly* were trying to hitch a ride downtown to Demonstration Area B in Grant Park.

Riding down Lake Shore Drive, we saw a little demonstration of 20 kids calling themselves "Spirit United" moving along the sidewalk holding signs denouncing Ticketmaster for over-charging credit card fees on rock concerts.

"Boy, these guys must be hard up for issues," I said.

"Just point me to the free-love booth. I never got in on that," the LA photog said.

Lame doesn't begin to describe Demonstration Area B. The Petrillo Band Shell in Grant Park entertained 150,000 people at the Aretha concert Friday night. A total of 12 people filled the seats Sunday to hear the Concerned Citizens Against Nuclear Incinerators. Professional vendors sold hemp handbags and tie-dyed T-shirts, but it just wasn't the same.

I looked out at the sailboats on the lake, the one million people gathered to watch Mayor Daley's Air and Water Show, and went home to rest up for **The Bobby Rush Midnight Skyline Boat Cruise.**

Of course, I remember Bobby as the only Black Panther who wasn't murdered in Chicago in 1969.

But others seem to think he makes a pretty good Congressman, a fine vice-chairman of the Democratic Party, a possible challenger in 1999 to Mayor Daley himself, and one very excellent party giver.

Bobby and Jesse Jackson Jr., the two young turk Congressmen from Chicago, rented the luxurious *Odyssey* cruise boat on Navy Pier and invited the Black Glitterati (courtesy of Ameritech, Comsat, First Chicago/NBD Bank, Commonwealth Edison, and TCI/Cable Television) for a champagne brunch shipboard from 11:30 PM to 3 AM on the eve of the convention.

The highlight of the evening -- what took me there -- was the gossip column leak that O.J. Simpson was going to show up with his old friend and attorney, Johnnie Cochran. Fat chance! I waited for two hours on the dock while the *Odyssey* re-loaded bands, hors d'oeuvres, liquor, and other essentials after having depleted supplies in an earlier cruise with the Indiana delegation.

The Hispanic Coalition gathered next door on the *Merri Dee II*, left dock and returned before Bobby started even taking names of people who wanted to come aboard.

I found myself leaning against a flower planter with my two new best friends, Kevin Antoine, 36, the Democratic Congressional candidate in the 4th District of Mississippi, and Gordon Bush, the Democratic Mayor of East St. Louis, Illinois, whom Bobby himself invited.

"I've been from here to there and back again," Gordon allowed. "Can you believe it, I must have a stack of 300 party invitations in my briefcase back at the hotel and I haven't even looked at them. I can't go to all these things. I started tonight at the Ameritech Blue Jeans Bash, went over to the Illinois delegation party at the Historical Society, stopped by David

Wilhelm's party (at The Park West), the Mayor of
Detroit's affair (in the Hyatt) and now I'm here because
Bobby himself invited me at the last party," he said.
"But I have to get back to the hotel. My wife is going
to kill me if I don't call in soon."

Kevin was more sanguine. "I'm here to do some
fundraising. I ran against a woman who everyone thought
would win, and I beat her in the primary. Al Gore came
down and endorsed her, but I beat her. In a district
that's 55% white, but 70% Democratic, I'm running
against a turncoat Democratic -- who switched over to
the Republicans last November -- so the party is all of
a sudden pretty interested in me."

I liked Kevin. He was wearing his own campaign button.
After three years as the Jackson (Mississippi) city plan-
ning director, he decided to run on a youth platform. **"I
know. I'm 36, but down there, you can be 55 and people
still introduce you as that young fella,"** he allowed.

Kevin was not looking forward to the cruise as much
as the 8 AM tomorrow opportunity to gather with
Mississippi's top Democratic fundraisers. Nonetheless, he
thought maybe Jesse Jackson Jr., the co-host, would show up
and he might convince him to speak on the black campuses in
his district - there are four in Jackson -- during the fall
campaign. But Jesse Jr. was nowhere to be seen.

Gordon Bush had a different problem. "I have to get
home and call my wife," he said. "Have you seen Bobby? He
invited me personal, and I want him to know I showed up."

136

"I'll tell you what," I told Gordon. "I'll take your picture here and you can just have Bobby call up my web site to confirm it."

"You can do that?" he asked.

"It's the 90's," I said.

"These boats are pretty remarkable," Gordon said. "You know anything about East St. Louis? We're right across from the Arch.

"When I came into office, we got ourselves one of these riverboat gambling casinos -- most remarkable thing you've ever seen -- and we're making $1 million a month tax revenues off of it. It's the largest riverboat casino in the world."

"How much is your annual city budget?" I asked.

"$18 or 19 million," he said. "So you can see, riverboat gambling has been good to us. When I got in office, we had tires falling off the police cars. We'd be scrunching to make payroll every week. And we had the highest per-capita murder rate in the country -- higher than Gary, higher than D.C. -- and the cops wondering every week whether they'd get paid to go out on the street. The crack dealers ran East St. Louis, but not any longer," he said.

"It's amazing what you can do in a city if you turn on the lights and put wheels on the police cars," I said.

"Yeah, riverboat casinos have been good to us," he said. "Our murder rate is down 25% and employment is up. I'm a casino fan."

"Sounds like you ought to order up two," I said.

"Well, it looks to me like they're not going to start to load until 12:30 AM," Kevin said.

"And Bobby Rush isn't even here," Gordon said.

"And O.J. is a no show," I said.

"I'm going to sleep," Kevin said.

"Me too," said Gordon.

"Me too," said me.

Coming Next: Part II
"Why Do You Think They Call It A Party?"

Why Do You Think They Call It A Party?

The first night of The Democratic Convention began on TV with a hall full of Democrats dancing the Macarena. This is going to be one tough week, I said to myself.

The Illinois Delegation, host to the convention, showed up late and missed the first roll call. "Were the parties too good to show up on time?" Bill Kurtis, the CBS anchorman in Chicago, asked a sheepish Miriam Santos, the Chicago city treasurer.

"They are really great parties, but parties are part of the process," she said.

Big Tommy, a man with whom I've been involved in several hotel and sports deals, called in after closing the Fairmont Bar with his new best friend, the saxophonist for Mark Russell's travelling minstrel show on PBS.

"I'm not going to make it," Big Tommy said. "I've been in the wrong place at the wrong time all week. I've got to get on your schedule, Stump. What's the next stop?"

"**The Comedy Central Party** at the Green Dolphin tonight," I said. "I have two tickets for Bill Bradley's 'Hoopla' over at Michael Jordan's. They say Phil Jackson is going to be there. But my money's on the Green Dolphin. The place only holds 700, and they have 1,600 names on the door list so far."

"How do you get on?" he asked.

"Oh that Deb! She can talk her way into anything," I said.

Deb is the vice president-general manager and my partner in <u>A Very Fine Video Post House on Webster Street</u> (<u>http://www.ipahome.com</u>). I watched her, earlier in the day, work the Comedy Central production manager over on the phone to get us on the list.

"In case there are any problems with the dubs of the show, our president would like to be on scene to resolve any difficulties," she lied. "And so would our scheduler, and our director of sales, and the editor, and you might as well put me on, too," she said. Deb rolled her eyes.

"**Are those all plus one?**" he asked.

"Sure, make them all 'plus one.' You can never have too much help," Deb said. She hung up the phone and raised her hand for a high-five. "We're in," she said.

The Green Dolphin had a pretty good spread of eats and beverages that Big Tommy, natch, was munching when I arrived. *Politically Incorrect,* the live wrap-up of the convention's first day with Al Franken and Ariana Huffington was playing on a video wall.

Old Plus One, my companion for the evening, worked her way back and forth to the hors d'ouerve table, reporting in on her celebrity sightings.

Roger Clinton, the president's brother, strolled in. Jim Carrey RSVP-ed he was coming, Plus One said, "and I stood right next to William Baldwin."

"Who's William Baldwin?" I asked.

"The actor," Plus One said, surprised at my ignorance. "He was in *Fair Game* with Cindy Crawford and is married to Chynna Phillips, the daughter of the Mamas and Papas. . . He's Alec Baldwin's brother!"

"Oh, Billy Baldwin. From the 47th ward," I said.

"Not everybody is from a ward in Chicago," she said. "How are you going to do cover this campaign, Stump, if you don't know who anyone is?"

"I'll take pictures," I said, "and people will see them on our web site and e-mail me with their names. Here, let me take a picture of you and that very fine editor, Marilyn Wulff,

who put together the Chris Dodd video for the convention,"
I said. "Now you take a picture of Stump with all his new best friends at the Comedy Central Party.  If this works, we'll use it tomorrow at JFK Jr.'s *George* soiree.

Coming Up: "Teamsters,Psychologists, and *George*"

Teamsters, Psychologists, and *George*

Tuesday was a full day. I was prepared to make my first appearance on the floor, stop by the trailers to say hello to Dan and Tom and Peter, and head off to John F. Kennedy Jr.'s *George* Party at the Art Institute. But before I could even go meet up with somebody important, I had to first find Big Tommy in Demonstration Area E outside the United Convention Center to swap out credentials.

We chose Demonstration Area E because, in the city lottery for protest slots, it appeared that the Teamsters Union and Psychologists United for Quality were double-booked from 6:45 to 7:45 for the only Demonstration Doubleheader on the agenda.

Demonstration Area E made Demonstration Area B in Grant Park look like a hotbed of anarchy. The Teamsters and Psychologists, all eight of them, showed up together because, it turns out, the county psychiatric workers have actually hired the Teamsters Union to represent them in negotiations with the Cook County Jail (and they are protesting the slow pace of the talks).

143

Despite this show of force, they were out-numbered by a dozen or more  freelance protestors in costumes who showed up as pigs, IRS file cabinets, Darth Vader, Richard Nixon, Craig Livingstone, and 12 Cuban exiles in ski masks.

Big Tommy was nowhere in sight. He was back to his old ways -- always in the wrong place at the wrong time -- and I diddled away the evening talking to the cops.

"What do I know about protests? I was four years old in 1968," one told me. "But hey, look at this new riot helmet they got me. My old one got busted when the Bulls won the NBA championship last June."

The *George* Party was another story. Kennedy's new political magazine, *George*, may look like a cross between *Details* and *Better Homes & Gardens* -- and it's web site (http://www.georgemag.com) is dull as dishwater -- but the celebrity of its publisher made "The George Party" the hottest ticket in town.

Originally planned for 400 of John-John's nearest and dearest friends, the guest list was expanded to 1,000 on the last day. I got on it through the good graces of Sugar Rautbord, the Kennedy's Chicago connection.

"Is that 'plus one'?" the list keeper asked.

"Yes," I said. "I'll be bringing along Old Plus One."

In the taxi on the way over, I told Plus One her job was to wait until John-John and I were in some intense conversation on foreign policy over brandy snifters, then casually snap a picture I could use with this story.

The Art Institute was a mob scene when we arrived. TV cameras as far as the eye could see, celebrity gawkers standing on the front steps, AIDS protestors holding a candlelight vigil behind police lines.

As we walked through the museum's antique armor collection, a line of servants in *George* T-shirts held out cocktails, wine, hors d'oeurves, and Perrier trays for our consumption. **Plus One grabbed for the eats and all but tossed the tray into some 15th Century Chinese exhibit case.**

"Whoa there, Plus One, I'm sure they'll be more food when we get to the real party," I said.

The party was held in the Art Institute's Central Garden, around the wading pool, under the glow of the famous Chagall windows. The first guests to find us, of course, were my celebrity-watching colleagues from the *Chicago Tribune* and *Sun-Times*, Jon Anderson and Bill Zwecker, and we exchanged witty repartee while the courtyard filled.

"I didn't RSVP today so I had to grovel to get in," I overheard Joel Daly, the Chicago ABC anchorman, complain to the person behind me.

"You know, if I was a star, I wouldn't show until after 10 o'clock," another society matron said. "Who wants people to think you don't care what happens at the convention?"

I was happily popping my eyeballs at every potentially important person I saw when an eagle-eyed woman named Karen Feld, of *Capital Connections*, popped me back.

"Hi, I'm Stump Connolly, the foremost political commentator on the internet today," I said.

"Oh really," she said. "I'm Karen Feld. I have a syndicated radio show and conduct a few chat lines myself. I have a homepage. The whole works."

We sized each other up, trying to determine who was telling the biggest lie.

"Were you in San Diego?" I asked. "How do you compare the parties in San Diego to Chicago?"

"San Diego wins hands down," Karen said. "I mean, how many art museums and historical societies can you throw a party in? When you cover eight to ten parties a night, like I do in Washington, you appreciate an occasional clambake or beach party."

"How'd you like the *George* party at the Republican Convention?" I asked.

"They did it all wrong," she said. "They held it at the San Diego Zoo -- which was overused to begin with -- and it just didn't work!"

"How are you enjoying this one?" I asked.

"I'm surprised there are no TV's. The convention is running late -- that's going to backlog the whole evening -- and I hear Chelsea and Hillary are coming later," she said.

Karen Feld surveyed the crowd and asked what I knew about them.

"This isn't a Washington crowd," she said.

"It's a Chicago crowd," I said.

"Sugar's bunch," she said snootily.

"I think Sugar Rautbord had a lot to do with it," I said.

"What's Sugar doing these days?" she asked.

"Same old thing," I said.

Realizing, of course, she had nothing in common with the nobody she was talking to, Ms. Feld moved on.

"I'll bet you're going to use that," Plus One said.

It would not be entirely accurate to say John-John sought me out to get my perspective on the convention so far.

I did speak with him briefly and Plus One got the picture, but the only thing Kennedy knows today that he didn't know yesterday is "Hi, I'm Stump."

My interest in the *George* party -- as an affair -- did not perk up until Plus One and I wandered over to the bandstand and discovered the entertainment was Poe, a Chicago-based rock band whose song "Angry Johnny" had been a struggle to get played on MTV.

<u>A Very Fine Video Post House on Webster Street</u> (http://www.ipahome.com) put together the rock video that, here in the confines of The Art Institute, was now the feature song at John-John's party.

Poe is the lead singer in the group, a straight-haired blond who appeared onstage in a black T-shirt that said "psycho," accompanied by electric cello player Cameron Stone, a bass guitarist in a lime-green sequin sportcoat, and a lead guitarist with this kind of tri-level yellow, red, and white haircut -- sort of like Dennis Rodman dressed up as a banana split.

(A lot of people, given the nature of political commentary these days, would skip any mention of the drummer for the sake of brevity. But I was a drummer myself -- I could play both "Bus Stop" and "Gloria" by the 10th grade -- and it seems to me also worth mentioning, even though I don't know his name, the drummer's pink double-barrelled bass and **cymbals with PASTE stenciled under the rims** were really cool, and when Poe turned around and banged 'em **like a mad woman in a gong factory,** it reflected the whole rhythm and hue of the universe, which is what drummers give to life: The Beat. **And she was pretty damn good at it.)**

A secret service agent in a dark blue suit, with a wrist radio and earpiece, and a goatee and an earring dangling a craw-footed peace symbol, came and stood in front of the stage watching the rooftops.

"Dang!" I said. "This is getting interesting."

A small coterie of Poe fans gravitated to the stage and swooned in front of Poe. Suddenly, across the wading pool and through the statues of four naked men peeing in the water, I saw Chelsea Clinton, the 15-year-old daughter of Bill and Hillary, making her way through the crowd. She had five of her school friends in tow and **some tall guy named Kevin Costner** (who I didn't know was available for babysitting gigs).

When Poe finished the last song in her set, the band started packing and I realized, belatedly -- and with many humble apologies to Plus One -- I'd blown all the prime celebrity watching time!

"Let's circulate," I said.

Inside the museum, a celebrity photographer was taking pictures of a celebrity person with a celebrity photo assistant picking at his hair.

"Who's that?" I asked.

"It's William Baldwin," said the guy with the instamatic blocking my view.

"Billy Baldwin again!" I said. "Why won't that guy leave me alone?"

149

"He likes to be called William," Plus One informed me.

Time was running short and, except for Billy Baldwin, I had delivered to Plus One no greater celebrity than Mike Royko (who was his usual garrulous self).

Out of the corner of my eye, I caught a glimpse of Laura, the assistant for Scrounger, my friend in the influence business.

"What are you doing here?" I asked Laura.

"Scrounger wanted to switch out some party tickets for tomorrow night, so I volunteered to come down. Besides, I wanted to star gaze like everyone else."

"So who you got?" I asked.

"I got Kevin Costner and Aretha and Roger Ebert and Oprah, of course. And Eleanor Mondale. Does she count?" Laura said.

"Barely," I replied.

"Who do you got?" she asked.

"I got Billy Baldwin," I said.

"Everybody's got Billy Baldwin. He's everywhere," Laura said.

A strange woman leaned over into our conversation. "I shook John-John's hand and met Christopher Lawford," she said. "Okay, I'm being a little gawky, shallow and insecure. But what the hell? It's fun."

At that moment, Chelsea Clinton brushed by with Costner in tow. Behind them, George Stephanopoulos held court with Rep. Barney Frank (D-Mass) and Norman Mailer sat at a table drinking scotch with Doris Kearns Goodwin.

"Oh, Kevin Costner and Chelsea," said our new best friend. "This is so much fun."

I turned to Plus One. "It's time to leave now. The amateurs are broadcasting."

We went out onto the Art Institute steps along Michigan Avenue. The minicam crews were gone, as were the protestors.

Standing on the sidewalk was a young photographer in a brown suit, with a box camera, an adjustable flash bulb, and what we used to call in the news game, a Pork Pie Hat.

"Take your picture, buddy?" he asked.

"Nice hat," I said. "Where'd you get it?"

"Phil 'n Phlash," he said introducing himself and handing over his card. "Phillip N. Phlash -- Public Eye" it said. I flipped it over. On the back it said "Harry's Velvet Room, 634 N. Clark."

"It's a chicks and cigars place," he said. "You want a good cigar? That's a place where you can get a good cigar.

"You want a good picture? You stand up there on the steps, and I'll snap you. If you'll give me your business card, I'll call you when it's ready," he said. "You only give me money if you like it. That's the way it works," he said.

"This is politics," I said, "you could donate the shot."

"This is life," he said."I'll give you a call."

Coming Up: "Dueling Parties."

Dueling Parties

"And you call yourself a journalist!" she said. "Where's the backup? Where's the proof? Why don't you even own a notebook? You go to a celebrity party with one roll of film? You can't go through life, Stump, taking notes on other people's business cards. Why even Phil 'n Phlash would do a better job of taking pictures. Why don't you call him?"

Well, Plus One was nothing but on my case Wednesday morning over the fact I'd only brought one roll of 24-shot film to the *George* Party.

"You know, you might be right," I said. "I really liked his hat."

Big Tommy was not in his office early the next morning, but he left me e-mail:

"I was there with the Concerned Teamster Psychologists, but couldn't find you. We'll catch up. Where's the party tonight?"

I e-mailed back: "Tonight is Dueling Democrats night. Chris Dodd and the Neville Brothers are entertain-

ing over at the Hard Rock, and the Celebrity Democrats
are gathering at Planet Hollywood. See you there!"

Just then, I got a call from Phil 'n Phlash. We
talked a while about our mutual interest in celebrities
-- "I got Billy Baldwin if you need him," he said."I
need Billy Baldwin like a hole in the head," I said --
and agreed to meet on the sidewalk outside Planet
Hollywood later to see if we couldn't work together.

"All right, Stump, I got my hands full with a 15-
month baby right now. And I mean that literally," he
said. "But I'll see you tonight. It's a big
city out there. Let's hit it."
The line clicked dead.

A funny thing happened on the way down to Planet
Hollywood. I was driving along Clybourn Street and this
city street sweeper pulled in front of me, which was
unusual because I'd never seen a street sweeper on
Clybourn, much less in the early evening hours, and it
was painted in the most pristine white I've ever seen on
a Chicago city vehicle.

I followed it for a couple blocks before I noticed
that, although all the brushes were turning, none were
actually touching the ground (You'd hate to ruin a good
paint job). So I followed it some more. For two miles!
And all the guy was doing was driving around downtown
Chicago pretending to sweep the streets. That's why
we call it The City That Works!

My diversion made me late arriving to the Celebrity Dems party at Planet Hollywood, which would not have been a problem were I on the guest list. But, of course, I was not.

Phil-n-Phlash was nowhere to be found. The closest approximation was a guy dressed up as the Sears Tower pointing a video camcorder at the klieg lights.

"We might have a problem here," I told Plus One.

"You mean we're not on the guest list?" she asked.

"Not exactly," I said, "but when I make a move, you follow."

A tall, gangly white guy named Luc Longley, the center for the Chicago Bulls, stepped into the guest line.

"Here we go, Plus One, stay close," I said.

Luc cleared the perimeter and I was halfway in behind him when Plus One actually looked at the person holding the list!

"And your name is--" she said.

"Michael Jordan," I said.

"Funny, you don't look like Michael Jordan," she said.

Back on the sidewalk, I told Plus One, "Let's try another entrance."

There is a restaurant next to Planet Hollywood called Wildfire and, I happen to know, both are cut out of the same Volkswagon dealership that occupied the prior space. "I have to go to the bathroom," I said. "So do you."

"I don't have to go to the bathroom," she said.

"Yes, you do," I said.

We slipped into the restaurant and through a couple glass-plated doors to a long, dark corridor that I hoped led into the other tenant's space.

I saw a guy with a red PRESS FLOOR PASS hanging off his neck and figured, hey, we're in.

"What are you doing here?" I asked.

"Sneaking in. What are you doing here?" he said.

"Sneaking in," I said. "But you have press credentials!"

"Not really," he said. "I have six floor passes for the convention, but they want a special white one with their logo on it for this party."

"It doesn't seem fair. What are you going to do?" I asked.

"Go to the bathroom," he said.

"It's back there," I said.

Plus One was pretty darned steamed when I suggested we move on over to the Hard Rock Cafe where Christopher Dodd, the chairman of the Democratic Party who had just this evening nominated Clinton for a second term, was throwing his party.

"Are we on this list, or are you just faking it -- again," Plus One said.

"We're in -- I think," I said.

In the line to register, the delegate behind us, who had just come from the Phillip Morris party at Dave and Buster's Video Game Parlor, pronounced it ". . .the pits. I never saw so few important people," he said.

"How'd they bill it?" said the guy behind him. "A tribute to Al Gore's sister?"

We walked to the entrance desk where computerized lists were collated into notebooks. I gave them my name.

"And this is?" she asked.

"Plus One," I said.

"Make sure you affix the bracelets to your wrist and don't lose them. The President may be coming later," she said.

"He's been following me all week," I said. "If we don't meet, can you give him my pager number?" I said.

"That's not under my control," she said.

Okay, I admit it. I had a great time at Chris Dodd's party at the Hard Rock. Very unpretentious, very straight-forward, very fun and very alive (even though most of the guests were from Connecticut).

The Neville Brothers were terrific. Al Franken, the author of *Rush Limbaugh is a Big Fat Idiot*, drew a big laugh when he announced that Chris Dodd was "well on his way to becoming the Haley Barbour of our party."

I was aware, as were most of the guests, that we were previewing a potential Democratic candidate for President in the year 2000. Who else is there? Al Gore? Dick Gephardt? Learn to say it slowly: President Dodd.

"Hey, there's Bob Schieffer from CBS," Plus One said.

"Well, well," I said, "I guess this is the party of the year."

Dodd bounced up onto the stage early -- not to dance but to thank the many little people who made the party happen. The names that caught my ear were James Carville, Dee Dee Myers, and George Stephanopolous, apparently moon-lighting on behalf of their favorite upstart.

Also of interest were the party's corporate spon-sors, which Dodd thanked profusely and included AT&T, Lucent Technologies, TT Trading, the Public Securities Association, J.P. Morgan Securities, Merrill Lynch, and United Technologies. You think Wall Street doesn't like The Neville Brothers? Wall Street loves the Neville Brothers -- especially if Chris Dodd does. Plus One went out into the crowd to find more broccoli, chicken stick-ers, and asparagus spears wrapped in prosciutto.

The Neville Brothers launched into their final song that ended in a rousing "Party. . . party. . . party. . . party. . . party." To which the crowd responded, "Four more years."

"You have to understand what's going on here," I told Plus One. "This isn't like the *George* party. The *George* party was all gawkers. People who wanted to see what it's like on the inside.

"These are the people who are on the inside. . . and they are partying down! They've been the outs and they've been the ins, and, on the whole, they've come to the conclusion it's more fun to be in."

"But it's so gross out there," Plus One said. "Just a bunch of political suits. You're afraid to rub up against them. It makes you feel greasy."

Coming Up: "The Worm Turns"

The Worm Turns

Oh, the turning worm that is politics. I woke up this morning to learn from the *New York Post* that the *Star*, a supermarket weekly, was about to break the story of the year-long affair Dick Morris, The President's top campaign strategist, carried on with a $200-per-hour call girl in a Washington hotel.

The tabloid report came with naked pictures, the girl's daily diary, and such juicy tidbits as the fact Morris called Hillary Clinton "The Twister" -- because of the havoc she caused -- but nonetheless wanted to have an affair with her if only she weren't married to Bill, whom he nicknamed "The Monster," because of his rage.

I called Phil-n-Phlash but got only his beeper number and a short explanation he was "on assignment." He's probably off chasing the B-girl, I thought -- God, I hope he found someone to watch the baby! His quick exit left me in the lurch.

Phil's wife, a concierge at the Sheraton Plaza, was my ace in the hole to get into Clinton's $1,000-a-plate post-speech gala Thursday night.

Without any real credentials, my best bet appeared to be showing up at the loading dock on Wacker Under, meeting Phil and walking in through the service elevator carrying flowers for the table centerpieces.

I thought the idea of Phil arranging our entry as busboys was poetically correct. But now, I would have to go in the front door. I hate that. That meant a call to The Scrounger.

I don't call The Scrounger often. She's a busy woman. In a former life, she was in the news business but was so successful at it, she stopped calling politicians and they started calling her. One favor begat another and pretty soon, The Scrounger became known around town as the person to call when you needed something important.

"How's it going?" I asked.

"I have to retire," she said. "I promised Gary Sinise I'd get him a floor pass to the convention tonight, now the whole Steppenwolf Theater Ensemble wants to go. Fortunately, *** ******* came up with three and **** ******** had another handful, but I can't get them a skybox! Those cost money!"

161

"Speaking of which," I said. "I need to get into Clinton's $1,000-a-plate gala at the Sheraton after his acceptance speech tonight."

"Good luck! It's a fundraiser," she said.

"Can you get me in as press?" I asked.

"I think another member of the press, particularly you Stump, is the last thing Clinton wants to see tonight," she said.

"Did you see the *Post?* I love how he told her there was life on Mars two weeks before NASA announced it. It's one thing to give head. It's another to give away state secrets. Why do they always have to show off to their bimbos?"

"Okay, what can you get me into?" I asked.

"Try the Democratic Leadership Council at Navy Pier. It's only a $75 ticket and they'll let you in on a press pass."

"My press pass is from 1976," I said. "I forgot to renew."

"It doesn't matter. This is the last day. Either they give the food to you or send it down to the mission," she said.

I was on my way out when Big Tommy called.

"I got a Perimeter Pass with your name written all over it" he said. "But you have to give it back. It's our only souvenir."

"Hell, I don't want to remember this convention," I said. "I want to forget it. But messenger it over. Maybe I can use it to parlay."

The thing I like about Perimeter Passes is they hang from your neck like they are official, but you can't tell what color they are: *i.e.* whether you are an important person or not. They do not actually get you into anything, but they are laminated, which is a big plus in the cheesy credentials game.

The Sheraton Plaza, where the president was staying, was a model of post-Olympics security. **Along three sides, the Chicago police had blocked off the street, strung yellow crime-scene ribbons and arranged blockades of garbage trucks and snowplows from one end of the block to the other.**

All pedestrian traffic in and out was funnelled through a narrow gate where FBI agents, police, and hotel security scanned every face and pocket.

I pulled my shirt cuffs out the ends of my suit, pinned a DNC souvenir button on my lapel, and held my Perimeter Pass up in front of my face. Here we go, I said.

I walked through the gate and into the lobby and up the escalator and turned into. . . The President's $1,000-a-plate Gala Post-Speech Celebration in the Sheraton Ballroom.

"And what table are you at, sir?" the waiter asked. I looked around. "Hey, what do you know, here it is right here. Table 239!" I said.

"Yes, 239," he said. "That's my table. Have a seat. I'm Kirby. I'll be your waiter."

Wait a minute. Isn't it supposed to be harder than this? Did we actually line up all these dump trucks here at taxpayer expense so some schmoe can stroll in off the street and just sit down for dinner with The President?

Should I go back out and try again, just to prove how easy it is? "No!" a little voice inside me said.

Democracy. Ah, I love it!

Only in America would The President of the United States, on this most intimate and personally rewarding night, throw on the feedbag with 3,000 total strangers just because they gave him $1,000 for the privilege of being in the same ballroom. Only in America can you take a wrong turn in a hotel lobby and have a waiter welcome you in to join The President's bash.

Only in America can you switch parties, gain the ear of The President, convince him to run for re-election on a "family values" platform, then get popped for banging a whore in a hotel all the while you were advising him.

Two women from Florida, both of whom I would char-acterize as thirty-something, blonde, Young-Republican types ("Barbie dolls in business suits," as C.C. Creams would put it) made the mistake of sitting down at my table.

"So," I said, "do you think Dick Morris should be hung from the nearest yardarm or tied to a rack and have baby food strained through his brain?" I asked. They excused themselves and moved away.

"You may start on your salad anytime," Kirby said "I'll be back with the wine."

The salad consisted of a single shrimp, curled on a leaf of bib lettuce, with a little red thing (it might have been a tomato) off to the side. It was covered in a dab of blended vinegar and oil that, in the supermarket, goes by the name "french dressing."

I ate one salad (in two swoops) and, since the table was devoid of guests, ate the one next to it, and the one next to that, and just about every other plate on the proverbial platter.

(Given the generous portions, given the $1,000/plate admission fee, I didn't for a moment think I was eating into the profits.)

A little after midnight, The President arrived from the convention hall where he'd just been renominated as the first sitting Democratic President since Franklin Delano Roosevelt.

"Well, uh, I can't believe we're all still standing," Clinton said.

And the hotel orchestra played some music, and my
new best friend, Kirby The Waiter, brought me another
bottle of wine, and, pretty soon, Thom, the town super-
visor from upstate New York and his friend Mark, a
public advocate in New York City, joined me at my table.

"So what brings you here?" I asked.

"I want to show my support for The President," Thom
said, "and meet some interesting people."

"Bad luck," I said. "I'm Stump Connolly, chief political correspondent of *The Week Behind*. This is my table."

Thom quietly ate his shrimp and wiped his chin.
This was not what he had in mind.

"How do you like the salad?" I asked. "Here, have
another. We got plenty."

A picture of a guy named Carl Lewis came up on the
video wall screens. And he said something. Then an
actress named Candace Bergen welcomed us all there. (And
Murphy Brown came up on the video wall screen saying the
very same words!)

And Al Gore and Tipper and Hillary said some
totally forgettable things. Finally, The President took
the podium and he thanked all the people who, at half-
past midnight, on the 4th day of partydom, were awake
enough to hear him.

"So tell me," I asked my new best friend Thom. "What's the biggest problem in Orangetown? Taxes too low?"

"You're kidding," he said.

"Yes I am," I said.

By this time, I'd worked my way through about $5,000 of Democratic food (five shrimps,five leafs of bib lettuce, five tomatoes, three 4-oz. butt steaks, three fish sticks, 18 beans, and 12 glazed carrots -- plus two bottles of wine) and the evening was dragging on like a trawler scraping bottom.

Through a day when crisis mounted on top of crisis, while Iraqi troops massed at the Kurdish border and network anchors tittered over the exploits of Clinton's chief campaign advisor, The President had stuck to the script. He bulled it out through his convention schedule, made all his appearances, hit all his talking points, and here, on the 4,200th and last party on the circuit, Bill Clinton showed that he wouldn't walk away from the table without collecting the last little nickel left in the kettle.

You'd think we'd get it by now. There is a vast and great divide in America between government and politics. The men and women we entrust to manage the nation, we elect through a process that bears no relation to their ability to govern.

Instead, we ask of them only that they perform well on TV, give us a good show, and make enough meaningless appearances at meaningless functions so they can raise enough money to do the same thing over again the next day.

No politician can break from the script he is handed. Because, the focus groups have decreed, the script will win, whether the politician goes along with it or not.

So Bill Clinton plays along, saying nothing of consequence, adhering to a "family values" script this evening written by a man who'd just stuck a whoopee cushion under the final line.

This election is Bill Clinton's to win or lose -- if only he can keep the worm on its belly.

When The President stopped talking, all the people around me stood up and started applauding. The band broke into a rendition of "Sweet Home Chicago":

> *Come on, baby don't you want to go,*
> *Come on, baby don't you want to go,*
> *Back to that same old place --*
> *Sweet Home, Chicago.*

Thom started to leave, but reached back to take a red rose off the centerpiece.

"Hey, that's stealing," I said.

"So sue me," he said.

"Okay," I said. "Just tell me one thing. Do you think the fact Clinton's campaign director was being blown seven ways on Sunday while he was advising The President will affect the election?"

Thom hesitated. He hemmed. He hawwed.

He had the makings of a good politician.

"It could," he said. "But probably not."

The Internet Ain't Ready For Reform

Somewhere between San Diego and Chicago, the Reform Party met in convention last month -- in Valley Forge, Pennsylvania, to be exact -- and I voted for Ross Perot. Three times.

I was one of the few to actually take advantage of the opportunity. Of the 1.13 million official Reform Party ballots mailed out, only 49,266 were returned to party headquarters by nomination day, with Mr. Perot receiving 32,121 votes and former Colorado Governor Richard D. Lamm, his opponent, getting 17,145 votes. The other 1,090,734 voters were either undecided or couldn't care less.

I was privileged to participate in Mr. Perot's nomination because I paused once long enough outside a supermarket to sign his ballot application form in Illinois (and wrote down my address legibly).

As a result, I received my official nomination ballot in the mail and, since Valley Forge was not on my travel schedule, I took advantage of the option of submitting my vote via the Reform Party World Wide Web Page.

It was reported in the *New York Times* that I was one of 11,000 people who cast my ballot via the internet. But the fact is, I was three of them, since I keyed my pin number in three times just before the midnight poll closing and the results were announced less than eight hours later.

I punched in the first time just to see if Perot's internet voting scheme worked. I punched in the second time to see if it could be tricked. And the third time to prove to myself no error message ("Sorry, this pin number has already voted twice.") appeared. **If I had had an extra five minutes, I probably could have punched in 50 or 100 times more and outvoted New Hampshire!**

To say that internet politics is an inexact science is to say the least. But it sure is fun. Any yahoo with an opinion can participate. And hold sway far out of proportion to his or her standing in the community.

Don't believe it? Consider this. A reasonably legitimate poll (conducted by *Hotwired*) of internet surfers one night asked visitors to name their favorite presidential candidate. The winner? Harry Browne, presidential candidate of the Libertarian Party.

The internet is a wealth of information for the political junkie. www.politicsnow.com -- the joint venture of the *Washington Post, Los Angeles Times, Newsweek*, the *National Journal* and ABC Television -- is a monstrously entertaining and informative site that contains such invaluable information as the daily tracking polls that guide campaign strategy. (And Bob Balaban's always fun *Buzz* column on the campaign trail.)

CNN and *Time* magazine publish allpolitics.com to recycle their material on the internet, and magazines like *Wired* and *Mother Jones* maintain sites (www.netizen.com and www.mojones.com) that offer some of the most insightful and interesting commentary you can find on Campaign '96.

For a single issue, *Salon* magazine (www.salonmag.com) had James Carville publishing his views under the title "Swamp Fever" but suddenly -- I don't know why! -- he seems to have slipped back into Clinton's campaign in a role formerly occupied by Dick ("The Dick") Morris.

There's not a candidate, or party, or special interest group that *doesn't* have a web site this year. And, as busy as The Stump has been just getting around to the goddamned parties, I've also tried to sample all of these well-intentioned efforts. And what I've discovered, believe it or not, is most are not all that interesting. Forget all the hoopla about so many millions of "hits," here are a couple examples that prove my point.

Example One: Politicsnow.com teased a feature before the Republicans met in San Diego called "The Virtual

Convention." It was going to be a online chat forum where voters from every state could join caucuses and discuss among themselves the important issues of the day.

Well hell, no one has more to contribute to that discussion than Stump. So I dialed in and took a seat, leaving this line of chat: "Welcome delegates! If no one has any objection, I am naming myself chairman of the Illinois delegation. See you on the floor. Stump."

Four days later, on the last day of the convention, the second registrant -- my fellow delegate -- signed in and said, "Why you?"

Example Two: The Democrats (also known as www.dnc96.org) decided to hold a daily chat conference (using I-chat plug-in software) with key figures in the Democratic party who would come by "live" and talk with their internet constituents from the convention floor.

First up, Walkin' Lawton Chiles, former Governor of Florida and frequent object of parody in Carl Hiaasen's *Double Whammy* novels.

Well, you'd hate to miss that. So I dialed in, downloaded the beta version of I-chat software, installed the plug-in in my Netscape browser, turned my computer off and on again, and waited five minutes for something to appear on the screen.

It must have been my mistake. I am, after all, just a lowly political correspondent. So I called back this week to see what I missed. Instead of chatting up a storm with Secretary of Labor Robert Reich, I downloaded the online chat session with Dan Fowler, the convention chairman, conducted just before the convention to inaugurate the service. (The only one that seemed to work.)

Here are my favorite excerpts from the log session:

Chairman Fowler says: Hello, welcome to the DNC chat room.

Mikeb says: Welcome, Mr. Chairman!
Chaim says: Hello, Mr. Fowler!
Chairman Fowler says: This afternoon we will spend a few minutes talking about the 1996 Democratic Convention that convenes one week from today and we will discuss the Presidential election or any other related subjects of interest to you.

Andrewperson says: Mr. Fowler, some say this convention shoud be as exciting as watching paint dry.
Chaim says: Help! I'm trying to get to the welcome room but nothing happens.
Mikeb says: How tough is it going to be to get everyone to take the "high ground" as the President encourages in spite of the rhetoric we heard last week.

Paul says: Chaim! You are already in the welcome room.
Chaim says: Oh.
Hazel says: Chaim! You're already here.
Chairman Fowler says: Political conventions are always exciting to those interested in politics. We will lead off on Monday night with an array of hosts, each of which will emphasize one of the

three themes of the convention: Opportunity, Responsibility, and Community.

Jochen says: How can I find out in which room I am in?
Hazel says: Jochen, type "look." Type: /look.

Gdangelo says: Even if supply-side economics works, in the global economy, the jobs would go wherever the economic advantage is greatest. Can we use this logic to show that our priority should be to increase the competitiveness of our workers?

Jochen says: look?
Hazel says: No./look.

Chairman Fowler says: Among our speakers Monday night will be Sarah Brady, who has been a gun control advocate for years. She is the wife of Jim Brady. And a Republican. Yet she will participate in our convention because the gun control issue is so important to the safety of Americans.

Minndfler says: Mr. Fowler, hello from Minnesota. Will we show America what a real, diverse party looks like?

Chairman Fowler says: Ron Brown, our great and good former chair and Secretary of Commerce, used to say that when you see the Democratic Party, you see the face of America.
Mikeb applauds wholeheartedly.
Paul applauds.
Minndfler cheers enthusiastically.

Jwilson says: Hey, Paul, it's Jeff. I thought you'd be in the air by now.

Kowen says: Test.

Flypusher says: I thought that Gov. Casey didn't get to speak more because he didn't back Clinton on the abortion issue.

Gdangelo says: Mr. Fowler, I believe the Republicans have a vulnerable position with supply-side economics because the jobs they would supposedly create could be in other countries now that we are in a global economy -- can we use this logic?

Stache says: Mr. Fowler, has Victor Morales of Texas been asked to speak?

Buttman looks for an ashtray.
Buttman blows smoke rings.
Edherlihy says: Good question on Morales.
Buttman says: Oops. Sorry, I was looking for the Dole-Kemp campaign.
Flypusher says: Mr. Fowler, will Mario Cuomo have a role in the convention?
Paul laughs at Buttman.
Ray grins at Buttman.
Buttman crushes cigarette and tries to make graceful exit.

Chairman Fowler says: President Clinton has advocated a middle-class tax cut for a long time. He proposes a $1,500 tax credit for the 13th and

*14th year of school, a $10,000 tax deduction for
a family to afford a college education for a
child, and a $500 tax credit for children under
the age of 12, to be phased out for families with
incomes of about $100,000. . . .*

And so on, and so on. Political discourse on the internet has a
certain wayward quality to it.

In all these "chat rooms" where the keyboard pundits converge, every sentence looks like it was written
with a tommy gun. Here's my opinion. Here's my opinion.
Superfly in Minnesota thinks this. You suck, Superfly!
Hi, is this the gay/lesbian chat forum or am I in the
wrong room?

This future, it's a wonderful thing. But waiting for
it to get to the internet can be a painful waste of time.

Follow the Money
Part 1

One of the expressions to fall into the political lexicon after Richard Nixon's disgrace in Watergate is Deep Throat's advice to Woodward and Bernstein of the *Washington Post:* "Follow the money."

There was little at stake back in 1972, except, of course, The Presidency of the United States.

But Deep Throat, whoever he was, knew that the oval office was purchasable and whoever put up the biggest downpayment, in all likelihood, got The White House along with it.

By today's standards, Richard Nixon's transgressions look like Pops Pankowicz nailed for a liquor store hold-up. In 1972, the total funds spent by the Richard Nixon and George McGovern in pursuit of The Presidency came to $104 million. This year, according to the *New York Times*, our two candidates for the President -- Bob

Dole and Bill Clinton -- are projected to raise and spend $600 million in their pursuit of the office.

They will, as a result of "election reform" measures instituted after Watergate, be given $150 million of this in taxpayer money to make the race. But, in 1996, that is just the base line cost of entry.

According to the *Times*, the parties will raise the other $450 million through a variety of election law subterfuges ("soft money") that include:

>$120-$150 million in individual and corporate contributions to each party.

>$25 million in contributions to each party's "host committee" for their summer conventions.

>$6 million in additional contributions to each party's campaign compliance committees.

>A $35 million separate campaign commercial fund established by the AFL-CIO.

>A counter-balancing $20 million fund by the U.S. Chamber of Commerce (to offset the labor ads).

>And an incalculable amount of "in-kind" office services, telephone fees, and other contributions from corporations, and individuals to unaccountable committees, entities and organizations who funnel contributions into campaigns that are, by law, barred from accepting them.

I myself couldn't be there, but the *Times* tells me
on September 12th Bill Clinton made up $3.5 million of
his campaign costs in a single night, in a single party,
at Harold Lloyd's former estate in Hollywood. The party
was hosted by Clinton's new best friend, David Geffen.
His second best friend, Barbra Streisand, sang the president a song and put the arm on her compadres for
$12,500 apiece to eat, drink, and shake hands with him
before giving a little private concert. All I can say is
Thank God Clinton didn't invite me. At the rate I was
going through shrimp in Chicago, I'd have been down
$50,000 before the second verse.

According to Common Cause, Hollywood has been very
good to the Democrats, contributing over $18 million to
the party in the last five years (versus $2.6 million
for the Republicans).

Within just the last 18 months, Geffen and his fellow executives and/or subsidiaries at Dreamworks SKG
gave the Democrats $525,000 in "soft money." Seagram &
Sons/MCA donated $620,000. The Walt Disney Company gave
$532,000, M&F Holdings/Revlon gave $536,250, and Goldman
Sachs, the Wall Street investment firm, skimped it out
with $510,000.

Not to be outdone, the Republicans found their top
angels in the tobacco and oil fields, and corporate
offices. Top contributors of "soft money" to the
Republicans include executives and/or subsidiaries of
Philip Morris, which gave $1,632,283; RJR Nabisco,
$970,450; American Financial Corporation, $794,000;

Atlantic Richfield (ARCO), $615,175, and United States
Tobacco, $448,768. When the final tally is counted,
even those numbers may
look like a pittance.

Top 50 Political Contributors

CONTRIBUTORS	DONATION	DEMOCRAT	REPUBLICAN
		IN MILLIONS	
PHILIP MORRIS	$ 2,741,659		
AT&T*	2,130,045		
ASSOC. of TRIAL LAWYERS of AMERICA*	2,106,325		
TEAMSTERS UNION*	2,097,410		
LABORERS UNION*	1,938,250		
INTL BROTHERHOOD of ELECTRICAL WORKERS*	1,821,710		
RJR NABISCO*	1,765,306		
NATIONAL EDUCATION ASSOCIATION	1,661,960		
AMERICAN MEDICAL ASSOCIATION*	1,663,530		
AM.FED. of STATE, COUNTY, & MUNIC. EMPLOYEES*	1,616,125		
UNITED AUTO WORKERS	1,592,298		
ERNST & YOUNG	1,590,215		
NATIONAL AUTO DEALERS ASSOCIATION	1,563,175		
FOOD & COMMERCIAL WORKERS UNION	1,510,395		
UNITED PARCEL SERVICE	1,479,581		
NATIONAL ASSOCIATION of REALTORS	1,408,233		
MACHINISTS/AEROSPACE WORKERS UNION*	1,396,375		
NATIONAL ASSOCIATION of HOME BUILDERS	1,338,049		
MARINE ENGINEERS UNION	1,317,165		
ATLANTIC RICHFIELD	1,278,678		
LOCKHEED MARTIN	1,272,153		
COMMUNICATION WORKERS of AMERICA	1,201,380		
GOLDMAN, SACHS & CO.	1,191,962		
JOSEPH E. SEAGRAM & SONS	1,190,200		
AMERICAN BANKERS ASSOCIATION*	1,122,909		

The scale markers (IN MILLIONS) read: $2.0 $1.5 $1.0 $.5 $0 $.5 $1.0 $1.5 $2.0

continued...

CONTRIBUTORS	DONATION	DEMOCRAT	REPUBLICAN
		IN MILLIONS	
AMERICAN FEDERATION of TEACHERS	1,088,384		
UNITED STEELWORKERS	1,087,150		
NATIONAL RIFLE ASSOCIATION	1,068,768		
AMERICAN INSTITUTE of C.P.A.'s	1,064,100		
BELLSOUTH	1,048,481		
MERRILL LYNCH	1,036,537		
U.S. TOBACCO	1,030,704		
CARPENTERS UNION*	1,008,816		
UNITED TRANSPORTATION UNION	1,006,600		
FEDERAL EXPRESS	996,975		
WALT DISNEY CO.*	968,072		
SHEET METAL WORKERS UNION	959,750		
MCI TELECOMMUNICATIONS	942,511		
LETTER CARRIERS UNION	933,199		
GENERAL MOTORS	930,568		
UNION PACIFIC	924,910		
TIME WARNER	913,175		
GEORGIA-PACIFIC	890,446		
DELOITTE & TOUCHE	860,314		
AMERICAN DENTAL ASSOCIATION	860,213		
ANHEUSER-BUSCH	844,720		
PAINEWEBBER	833,767		
ENRON CORP.	829,566		
LORAL CORP.	823,300		
NATIONAL BEER WHOLESALERS ASSOC.	812,242		
TOTALS	$63,728,356	$35,277,904	$28,326,93

* Contributions made by more than one affiliate or subsidary

(Compiled by the Center for Responsive Politics from Federal Election Commission data for contributions from January 1, 1995, to June 30, 1996. Includes 'soft money' to national parties, PAC donations to candidates and individual contributions to all Federal Candidates from a company, its affiliates and/or subsidiaries. * Reported December 26, 1996, in the *New York Times*.)

Why do the big givers give?

"Politicians and movie stars spring from the same DNA," Jack Valenti, chairman of the Motion Picture Association of America, the movie industry's trade group, told the *New York Times*. "Both hope for applause, read from a script, and hope to persuade audiences."

Darienne Dennis, director of communications for Philip Morris, says, "Philip Morris supports those who share our thoughts. We have a responsibility to our employees and shareholders to be in the political process and we are happy to do so."

Gerald Lowrie, senior vice president of Government Affairs for AT&T, which split $743,000 almost equally among both parties says, **"Government can change how you live and how you work. If you ignore who is in office, it can be at your peril."**

Presidential elections today operate on such a grand scale, it is hard to find the quid pro quo that turns a $600,000 contribution into a bribe. Bribes are things handed to aldermen in envelopes in exchange for zoning variances. Occasionally, a Congressman or Senator's vote for or against a certain piece of legislation can be traced to a certain large contribution from someone in his district. But how do you link Bob Dole's waffling on tobacco bans to Philip Morris' $1.6 million Republican contribution (especially when they gave $370,000 to the Democrats at the same time)?

Politics and money. It's all just sort of a big coincidence on the presidential scale. Ask the campaign finance chairmen.

"I personally, would like to see campaigns cost less money and run for a shorter period," Howard Leach, finance chairman of The Republican Party, told the *Times*. "But since our opponents are running an expensive campaign, we have no alternative but to buy high-priced media like they do."

"There's no question there needs to be changes in how campaigns are financed," said David Eichenbaum, communications director for the Democratic National Committee. "But until the overall system is changed, we are not in a position to say 'we won't raise money.' We want a level playing field."

We've heard that one before. Wasn't it only ten months ago, at a citizen's forum in New Hampshire, that Bill Clinton and Newt Gingrich clasped hands and promised to reform political campaign financing?

Nothing has changed. And no one has tried very hard to change it (except maybe Ross Perot, who is taking $29 million himself in federal money this year to run). If anything, the situation is getting worse.

What started in 1974 with the simple promise of federal campaign support to candidates who agreed to limit individual contributions to $1,000 (and corporate contributions to $5,000) was quickly subverted by the exemption for industry, labor, and lobbying groups who formed Political Action Committees.

Another exemption allowing unlimited contributions to state and national parties for "Get Out The Vote" campaigns became, in 1979, the source of new-found "soft money." A loophole allowing unlimited contributions to Federal Election Commission "Compliance Committees" opened another avenue for $12 million in giving.

Convention "Host Committees," whose activities are allegedly unrelated to the party, weren't conceived of when the law was written. So things like Ameritech's $1.2 million tab for underwriting half the parties at the Democratic convention in Chicago doesn't even go into the calculations. Recent rulings in the Supreme Court, moreover, allow "issue campaigns" and "get out the vote" efforts by the Christian Coalition, AFL-CIO, Chamber of Commerce, and Sierra Club to spend unlimited amounts outside the FEC limits.

Federal election spending limitations are a sham and a fraud. As Max Frankel recently pointed out in his *New York Times Sunday Magazine* column, the average Senate seat now costs at least $5 million to win, and sometimes as much as $30 million; a seat in the House of Representatives over the same six years has to be contested three times, at a cost that can also reach $5 million.

"Attempts to restrain and reform our campaign financing have failed disastrously," Frankel wrote. "The people in power have mastered the system and however much they dislike it, they mistrust all change. Those too disheartened by all the extortion just quit. On the way out, Senator Bill Bradley says that 'you can't change anything until you deal with the money in politics;' Senator Alan Simpson says that money is 'poisoning the system, it is prostituting ideas and ideals.'"

So what happens to all that money? How do you spend $600 million running for president?

See Follow The Money - Part II. Coming Monday.

Follow the Money
Part 2

Fortunately, I have friends in advertising. I know people who measure impressions, who call their clients "brands" (and themselves "brand managers") and calculate, every day, what it costs an advertiser to buy a vote of confidence.

Friends like these come in handy around election time. They help to understand the rawest form of politics, the merchandising of a candidate.

It's not a game I have pursued, but one I admire quite a bit. So I am disappointed this year to see the quality of the political commercials hitting the air. There are no Willie Hortons, no Mornings in Americas, no Men from Hope, no daisies exploding in atomic bombs.

It's slam and be slammed. Tit for Tat. Buy versus Buy. Market-to-market trench warfare. Even your detergents are kinder toward their rivals.

Throughout 1996, a research firm named Competitive
Media Reporting (http://www.usadata.com) tracked all
U.S. campaign spending on television and radio advertising for all presidential, Senate, and House candidates,
as well as issue campaigns. Their records are taken from
the station ad log books based on the advertiser of
record. Their January - November totals are as follows:

	TELEVISION	RADIO
DOLE FOR PRESIDENT	$32,858,000	$2,333,100
CLINTON FOR PRESIDENT	28,877,700	1,530,200
PEROT FOR PRESIDENT	17,241,300	3,525,400
All Other Presidential Candidates	7,034,900	909,100
Republican Natl Committee	24,924,600	839,500
Democratic Natl Committee	22,886,300	380,300
Republican House/Senate Campaign Committees	-0-	736,200
Democratic House/Senate Campaign Committees	-0-	54,000
All U.S. House Candidates	56,176,400	4,670,600
All U.S. Senate Candidates	75,487,400	3,178,600
All Other Local Races/ Propositions/Issues	127,768,500	25,698,000
TOTAL ALL POLITICAL (Excluding Union)	$393,255,100	$43,855,000

(In the original version of this story, published in early September, 1996, Stump reported that the January to June tally for TV spending was $12.5 million for Clinton, $9.4 million for Dole, and $5.5 million for the other Republican contenders.

("Although there are no numbers available for July, August and September or October," I wrote, "in the last presidential campaign, in the single month of October, 1992, CMR tracked television advertising buys in network and spot TV for Bush of $28 million; Clinton, $26 million; and Perot, $32.5 million. With inflation and record campaign contributions, experts like Dr. Herb Alexander, head of the Center for Political Integrity, predict presidential spending this year may be as much as 50% higher."

(Boy, did we guess low! In his post-election memoir, Behind The Oval Office, Dick Morris boasted that the Clinton campaign and DNC "at the behest of the president" spent upwards of $85 million on TV ads.

("Week after week, month after month, from early July, 1995, more or less continually until election day in '96, sixteen months later, we bombarded the public with ads," Morris wrote. "The advertising was concentrated in the key swing states: California, Washington, Oregon, Colorado, New Mexico, Louisiana, Arkansas, Tennessee, Kentucky, Florida, North Carolina, New Jersey, Pennsylvania, Ohio, Michigan, Wisconsin, Illinois, Minnesota, Missouri, and Iowa. During this period, television viewers in these states saw, on aver-

age, 150 to 180 airings of a Clinton or a DNC commer-
cial, about one every three days for a year and a half."

(It's an odd admission, even for a disbarred politi-
cal strategist, because if CMR, using station advertiser
logs can only find $12 million in TV spending prior to
July, the question arises: who bought the rest?)

I asked my old friend Half Dead Mitch, who used to
handle media buying for Philip Morris (and fell too much
in love with their products) how that compares to some
of his more commercial clients.

"It's obscene. Totally obscene," Mitch said. "These amateurs are ruining the business."

"Look what they are doing to McDonalds. McDonalds is
The #1 Advertiser on television every October. In 1992,
they spent $32.4 million on network and spot TV. In 1994,
they spent $34.8 million. In 1995, it was $34.7 million.

"This year, because they are pushing Arch Deluxes,
McDonalds will try to spend $35 million and they won't
be able to find the time because the politicians have
gobbled it all up.

"Some guy decides he wants to be president of the
United States," Mitch said, lighting a Marlboro. "What
does he do? He hires his best friend as the campaign
manager because they've been dreaming about this since
they ran him for prom king together in high school.

"They rent an office in Washington for too much money; hire a couple political consultants who've been down this road before; and get their poombah friends in the media to call them "The Front Runner" in the race to The White House.

"The first thing the consultants tell them . . . because they've been down this road before. . . is raise more money. You never can have enough money. So they spend a year getting their war chest together and what do they do? They blow it all in 30 days of primaries in the Spring. Look at Bob Dole. He raised and spent $37 million by April."

"But he won," I said.

"Yes, and that's when he got in trouble." Mitch said, "You see, the game changes when you get the nomination. You have to start acting professional. Now you have "The Party" behind you. That gives you another $150 million to play with. But it's not really FREE MONEY because The Party comes along with it.

"The party has *its* consultants, and *its* headquarters, and *its* whole apparatus to manage, and everybody else in the party is leaching money out of the guppy's belly to run their own races for House, Senate and Governor seats. So instead of having some professional advertising guy decide how to launch the product -- I mean, the candidate -- you have 100 people deciding, and the decision is to spend it everywhere.

"And the money kind of leaks away all summer -- with everybody getting their own little piece of it -- so when the Dole handlers sit down to finally pick whether to run him as a tax cutter, or drug buster, or man of honor, there's no ready cash available."

"But the race hasn't started yet. Traditionally, political campaigns don't begin until Labor Day," I said.

"Precisely," Mitch said. "And here's where Bob Dole blew it again. Every campaign has some twist that differentiates it from the one before. In 1992, Clinton won because he had his rapid response team. In 1994, the Republicans took back Congress using some crafty issue-advertising the Democrats didn't catch on to until it was too late.

"Clinton's trick play this year -- and he used it quite well -- was summer advertising. Because he didn't have any primary foes, he was swimming in money. So he bought TV time all over the country, in targeted districts, and ran these kind of softie maintenance ads to keep his tracking poll numbers up.

("In my opinion, the key to Clinton's victory was his early television advertising," Morris would later write. "There has never been anything remotely like it in the history of presidential elections.")

"Because Clinton was on the air, Dole had to go on the air. Dole went chasing the tracking polls. And he didn't have a clear message so he frittered away a million here and couple million there. By the end of

191

the summer, Dole's aides are telling him his TV message is "unfocussed."

"So what does he do? Fires the
advertising team! Just when Dole
should be pulling the trigger, he
decides to clean the gun."

"Okay, Mitch, so let's say Dole comes to you. He's
out of money, has no message, and only 45 more days
until the election. What do you do?"

**"Here's the beauty of what you call a political process,"
Mitch says, "he's not out of money.**

"On August 30th, one day after the Democratic convention ends, we the taxpayers give Dole $74 million.
And we give Clinton $74 million. And, just to show what
kind of sports we are, we give Ross Perot $29 million in
Federal Election Commission matching money.

"Do you know what that's going to do to the TV
spot market this October? You know my client,
McDonalds, who's spending $35 million to pump burger
sales on TV? My guess is Clinton and Dole each will
spend $40 million in the same period. And Ross Perot
will hop onboard with a $20 million buy. **That's $100
million -- $15 million more than McDonalds, Wendy's,
Burger King, Taco Bell, and Pizza Hut combined will
spend on October television commercials.**

"In a good year, with the football season in full
swing and an exciting World Series, Budweiser will only
spend $10 million in October. Those ads you see for

Chevy Blazer Trucks only eat about $12 million of
October airtime. Even the big image advertisers -- AT&T,
Sprint, and MCI -- won't go above $22 million for TV
spots in October.

"These guys who run for President and all their
little helpers who run for Representative, Senator or
Governor from some state somewhere dropped about $180
million into the TV market four years ago. This year,
it's looking like the overall political buy for federal,
state and local office this October could be around
$300-320 million. For what? . . . air. . . and what
exactly are they selling?"

"So what do you tell Bob Dole when he comes to you
for advice?" I asked.

"Get a life."

"No, seriously," I said.

"Okay, seriously," he said.

"Politicians are meat. You buy politicians based on how fresh they look, how hungry you are, and whether you can afford them.

"You know how Carville was quoted in '92 saying
'It's the economy, stupid?' He was right. It's always
the economy. Voters vote because of pocketbook issues.
All of this junk political advertising out there, this
wash of imagery, pro and con, back and forth between the
two camps, is confusing voters.

193

"Bob Dole's got one chance in this election," Mitch said. "He should go on the air and make himself indispensible to the voters."

"How does he do that?" I asked.

"Coupons," Mitch said. "It's the bread and butter of advertising.

"You think people go to McDonald's to buy Arch Deluxes because of the way the sun sets over the arches in the commercials? They go because it's a Value Meal special for $1 off, and you can Super Size it for only 39 cents more."

"I'm not sure I'd spend 39 cents to Super Size Bob Dole," I said.

"You're missing the point here. Bob Dole has to go on television and offer people something of value," Mitch said. "He has to do it in such a direct, startling, bare bones way that people see some practical advantage in going to a polling booth and pulling the lever for him."

"And you say that's coupons?" I said.

"Works for me," Mitch said. "He dumps the whole TV ad campaign, saves up the $74 million, and tells people during the next debate he'll give them each a dollar if they take their voter stub, write "I voted for Bob Dole" on the back and send it to him.

"Hell, this could be the best thing to happen to voter registration since the civil rights movement."

"Don't you think that's a little crass?" I asked.

"We're talking politics. You can't be too crass. It's the only way to return sanity to the process."

The Talk of Naperville III: The Debate

Lucy's Mother is not the only home nurse specializing in cancer recovery therapy living in Naperville. There are half a dozen others -- and although her new condo is nice, it is not as nice as the other housing in this Republican-leaning, high-tech corridor of Illinois.

Lucy's Mother is not an easy woman. Divorced twice, with eight children, she is 59 years old, single, and a home-care nurse living in Naperville.

When the presidential debates came on TV last Sunday, I sat down to pot roast and potatoes with Lucy and her mother to watch. Ted Koppel has his on-air focus group wired to sensors in hotel rooms. I have Lucy's Mother, my "focus woman."

"Ninety minutes! Lord, what are they going to talk about for 90 minutes?" Lucy's Mother said. "Are you going to put some coffee on? I'm going to have trouble staying awake."

Chosen by coin toss to go first, President Clinton opened with a few nice remarks about his opponent and a defense of his presidential record. Dole, coming next, looked tan and rested.

"What do you expect? He's been on vacation in Florida," Lucy's Mother said.

Dole took special notice in the audience of his wife Liddy, daughter Robin, and Frank Carafa, "who pulled me out of the mountains of Italy a while ago" -- when Dole was wounded in World War II.

"How many times are we going to hear that one?" she snapped.

"I learned from them that none of us can go it alone," Dole said dead on, and humbly, into the camera.

"Now that's a twist!" she said. *"I didn't expect that."*

"I have run against the odds for a long time and I will continue to run -- with your help," Dole said.

Lucy's Mother leaned forward listening. She wanted to help. *"Slow down, Bob."*

"He always does this. He talks too fast," she said. *"I mean, he thinks too fast and he tries to talk fast enough to keep up with what he's thinking, so he loses it. He talking slower tonight, that's good."*

Dole and Clinton, answering questions posed by PBS anchorman Jim Lehrer, sparred back and forth for the next 40 minutes over medicare, tax cuts, the war on drugs, and campaign finance reform. Lucy's Mother pulled out her knitting and stitched, saying little.

In time, Dole picked away at Clinton looking for chinks in the president's armor. Lucy's Mother looked up.

"You know what Dole's doing." "He's acting like a naughty grandpa lecturing the kids. He's done pretty good so far, but I think the Prozac is wearing off. If he gets nasty, I'm getting turned off."

Dole opened the door for a discussion of the Israeli crisis, and Clinton closed it. Dole outlined a school voucher proposal, and Clinton reminded him vouchers would drain federal money from the 90% of American children who attend public schools.

Lehrer, the moderator, threw up a hanging curve to Dole, asking for his reflections on the president's character. Dole let it pass. But knowing he needed to say something negative, he accused Clinton of being a "liberal."

"He's not a liberal, he's a centrist," she scolded.

"Whenever they're in a tight race, the Republicans drag out this liberal charge," Clinton responded, with, "It's sort of their Golden Oldie."

"Whoooeee, Bill, get mad!" Lucy's Mother said.

Lehrer raised the question of Whitewater and Lucy's mom said, "Here's where Clinton gets to say: forget the past." But Dole persisted in pressing Clinton over possible pardons for his friends who've been indicted.

"He's trying to get Clinton to say something about Whitewater. Just let him keep talking, Bill," she said, as if Clinton had invited her onstage as his personal advisor. **"The clock is running out. Dole's losing it. He's going into his old man thing, throwing everything he has at the fan. He peaked too soon."**

Clinton concluded with a recitation of the reasons why he believed Americans were better off than they were four years ago.

Dole took his last opportunity to "address the young people of America" inviting them "to tap into my home-page, www.dolekemp96.org."

"I thought he said tap into his old age," Lucy's Mother laughed. *"Dole's not old because of his age, he's old because he doesn't know who he's talking to."*

The debate dissolved into the usual mix of handshakes and commentary. We turned the sound down.

"Dole said all the right things, but he didn't educate me and he didn't sway me," Lucy's Mother said. *"I'm for Clinton. On Medicare alone. And this didn't change my mind."*

"Are you better off now than you were four years ago," I asked her, echoing Clinton's theme.

"Am I? No. My money's not worth as much as it was, but I'm just a common person," she said. "Other people probably are."

"Did anything surprise you?" I asked.

"That thing Dole said at the beginning about none of us can go it alone. That didn't sound very Republican, and I think he meant it," she said. "It's like the Republicans and Democrats have flip-flopped this year."

"Are debates worthwhile?" I asked.

"This wasn't a debate. It was a discussion. If they wanted a debate, they would have had to let everyone in. Then you could have heard all sides," she said. "I think they should have let Perot in. They wouldn't have been able to control the conversation this way if Perot were in it."

"There's going to be a third party, you know. It's just a matter of time. Perot won't be it. He attracts all the kooks. But this election -- it's a horrible process. Maybe we should just have a king and queen. Wouldn't that be fun?"

Twenty-one minutes after the debate ended, ABC News came on the air with an instant poll of its sample audience showing 50% of 616 voters thought Clinton won the debate, 29% thought Dole won and 19% thought the debate was a tie.

The more important hidden statistic in the ABC poll was that, of all those responding, 95% said the debate would not change their opinion of who should be president. Let's give all the media their statistical due.

With an alleged 90 million people watching the debate on ABC, NBC, CBS, PBS, and CNN, a voter registration fig- ure of 52%, a statistical probability that 45% of the TV audience was under the voting age of 18, a projected turnout on election day of 54%, and ABC's polling results, with a margin of error of 4.5%, it's quite likely that only one-half of one percent of the voters who saw the presidential debate, or **69,500 people**, will vote for someone other than the candidate they favored before it started.

Is Lucy's Mother one of them?

"I remain unconvinced. I guess I'll just hold my nose and vote."

Then she folded her knitting, and went home.

Free TV

We must be careful what we wish for. . . because we just might get it.

I feel this week, as I watch the array of free TV time given over to this fall's electoral candidates, a certain remorse over why we let these yahoos run for office in the first place.

On the local PBS station, there is a half hour each night devoted to 2-minute presentations from the various Congressional candidates in Illinois.

"I am a teacher at New Trier and I want to show my students why it's worthwhile to oppose a sitting congressman who's 87 years old and can't sign his name to an absentee ballot," one says; *"I'm a little league baseball umpire and, although I've never run for public office, I think I have what it takes to be fair,"* says another.

On the Fox Network, Rupert Murdock has given Clinton and Dole a minute a night in primetime to address the public with no invoices forthcoming from his sales department.

On the CBS Network News -- and all 14 CBS-owned television stations and 21 CBS-owned FM radio stations -- Clinton and Dole are getting 2 and a half minutes a night to address four topics chosen by a CBS News poll.

Their answers will be broadcast inside the *Nightly News*, rebroadcast on the local station's 10 PM newscast, on the network's *Up to the Minute* overnight news, inside the *Morning News*, and, at least three times a day, on CBS radio.

The ABC network is working on a plan to give Clinton and Dole a free hour in primetime the week before the election, and NBC has offered its own chunk of time inside *NBC Dateline*.

These offers, of course, have not been extended to Ross Perot who will, one presumes, just go out and buy his own time or, if he is smart, get on the horn to Murphy Brown -- where there's still an audience for his kind of schtick -- and book himself into a cameo.

The network acceptance of giving away free time to presidential candidates is a tribute to Paul Taylor, a former *Washington Post* reporter who founded the Free TV for Straight Talk Coalition earlier this year.

Last March, Taylor convinced a number of leading journalists, most prominently Walter Cronkite, to sign a full page ad in the *New York Times* advocating 2 minutes of public airwaves be given over to each candidate on every licensed station for unadulterated, uninterrupted "straight talk" on issues.

In the long run, it is Taylor's hope that the Free TV formats developed this year will replace the slick commercials and packaged news interview/debates that characterize current elections.

In point of fact, the campaign handlers have outsmarted us again.
A diligent search of the airwaves has shown Murdock's free air is neither advertised or easy to find (unless you are waiting for a rained out World Series game).

NBC buried its first airing of the Free TV spots between a guess-the-year trivia contest and Rosie O'Donnell's profile in *Dateline.*

PBS, which has more air than audience, had little trouble breaking open time at the end of *The Lehrer Hour*, but got little more than leftovers from the CBS taping.

It is to CBS's credit that the network not only gave over more free time to the candidates than anyone else, but did it the spirit and substantive manner that Taylor's coalition envisioned.

In the four areas of Education, Taxes, Social Security & Medicare, and Health, CBS presented Dole and Clinton, *mano a mano*, in a "first person, unedited" presentation of their messages.

Dan Rather promoted it at the beginning of the broadcast, introduced it with a proper, but not over-hyped explanation of the ground rules, and concluded, after the candidates finished, ". . . and that's a part of our world."

Civility, logic, argument, and persuasion can be a part of our national discourse. The candidates -- both Dole and Clinton -- presented themselves well in the context. And it was a context that held up well against what we in the news biz might call "competitive formats," *i.e.* "The Debates."

Why do we feel it necessary to give over 90 minutes of prime entertainment time to political candidates who use the occasion to: (a) telegraph their punches; (b) turn any question into a platform for a rehearsed response; and (c) know, even before they go in, how they will "spin" the results? That's not entertainment. That's not even politics. That's propaganda.

The beauty of Taylor's solution is that it recognizes propaganda is at the very heart of the political process. One side believes in certain principles; the other side holds to its own. The job of the candidates is to put forth their positions cogently, in arguments we can understand, in a time frame that recognizes we, the people, have more important things to do than listen to two automatons blow smoke up each other's ass.

There are two more points that should be made about our experiment in Free TV this year: How the candidates responded, and how the process did, and will, affect political discourse in America.

How did the candidates respond? About as you would expect. Clinton, denied the trappings of the Oval Office, sat himself down in front of an antique dresser that looked just like the Oval Office. Dole, having no

Oval Office to fall back on, put up a flag next to a bookcase and made it look like the Oval Office.

Clinton wore a patterned dark tie; Dole wore a bright red tie. Dole went with the wide shot open and slowly rotating zoom in; Clinton started close and got closer.

If ever there were an example of candidates staying on message, this was it. I didn't hear a word, a phrase, a joke or an aside, that I hadn't heard before. Dole leaned back; Clinton leaned forward. Clinton did better, somehow, not because of anything he did, but because, somehow, he is. America learned that. And it was a good lesson that will be confirmed on Election Day.

How did Free TV affect the political process this year? In a year dominated by the influence of money on politics, the campaign handlers determined that Free TV -- surprise -- would save them money.

The *New York Times* reported on October 22 that of the 31 commercials Clinton has broadcast since 1995, 26 have been "attack" or "either/or" spots; while only 5 have been "entirely positive," including three in the last month.

In the ebb and flow of elections, here's a tip from Inside: Campaign handlers think 14 days ahead of the media reaction, what they call "The Unveiling." That is the amount of time it takes for handlers to secretly plan their state-by-state, market-by-market media buy, select by focus groups a resonant theme, and buy enough Gross Rating Points (GRP's) to convince the public they are right.

Let's assume the most efficient political machine in the world is working on behalf of one candidate or the other these last 10 days.

If the tracking polls tomorrow (Saturday) say "Bob Dole can pick up 15 points replacing Jack Kemp as his VP candidate with God," the handlers still can't get into an editing room to make the spot until Sunday; they can't get it Fed Ex-ed to 200 TV stations until Monday, clear "continuity" until Tuesday so, if air time has already been bought, **they cannot start airing the spot until Wednesday so it will be at least Thursday before the tracking polls tell them whether God even plays as a running mate.**

The fact is, from this point forward, the media game is over. What's been bought will be filled. What's not will be given back to McDonald's.

If you are a professional political handler (and who isn't?), you know the way to play the last 10 days of the campaign is split your ad buy 50-50 with nega-tive/positives the week before the end, and throw up your positives 100% the weekend before the voters vote.

How did Free TV affect all this? The handlers were, as one might suspect, skeptical about Taylor's initial plan. But they knew that if CBS, PBS, Fox, NBC, and ABC were willing to give over what would otherwise cost them $20 million for primetime exposure, they could change the mix -- as Clinton did -- to 75-25 negative/positive, and still appear to be running a positive campaign.

And you bought it. You suckers!

There's no one lower on the food chain of political
television advertising than the viewers. But you also
had a glimpse of what might have been.

And if you want to see more,
send CBS a letter saying
"Congratulations. And thank you."

It's hard to lead.

Sugar and Politics

Politics is an interesting diversion. We find ourselves one week saying, "Hmmm, this is odd, why are the Florida Sugar Farmers the #7 political advertiser on TV in America this year?" and then, only a few days later, saying "Who gives a shit about a bunch of alligators anyway?"

Who gives a shit? Some very rich people, it turns out, give a pretty God damned about alligators and they are willing to spend more to pass or defeat a penny-a-pound sugar tax amendment to the Florida Constitution than most states will spend electing a Governor this year.

The amendment -- actually three, put forward by The Save Our Everglades Committee -- would create a "penny a pound" tax on Florida sugar to go toward clean-up of The Florida Everglades.

It is one of six referendums on the Florida state ballot this November -- another, sponsored by the Sugar Farmers, would require ballot referendums affecting the constitution get a two-thirds majority -- and the source of one of the strangest, and most expensive, political donnybrooks in America this year.

The battle pits a New York stock broker -- wanting to honor the legacy of his retired fishing buddy and dead neighbor -- against the two largest sugar companies in America in a contest that, at the end of the day, will cost the three of them at least $20 million to resolve in the electoral arena.

Now, sugar and politics are no strangers in the nation's capital.

Over the last 25 years, the federal sugar subsidy program has been one of the most egregious examples of "corporate welfare" in Congress. With guaranteed price supports 20 to 23 times higher than corn, wheat or soybean programs, American sugar farmers receive about 22 cents per pound for their product in America while the price on the world market hovers closer to 11 cents per pound.

As a result, the U.S. General Accounting Office has determined, American consumers pay $1.4 billion more a year to support their sugar habit than they should and 42% of the direct federal subsidy goes to less than 1% of the sugar farmers, namely the Florida Crystal/Flo-Sun Company, and U.S. Sugar Corporation.

The sugar subsidy program survives through import quotas and price supports enacted by a Congress that, between 1979 and 1994, received $12 million in sugar grower political contributions.

If sugar farmers were a large and vast voting block in America, Congress might be forgiven its willingness to bow to the constituency. But the fact is there are only about 130 major sugar farmers in America, most located around Lake Okachobee in the Florida Everglades, and Flo-Sun and U.S. Sugar control over 70% of the 1.8 million tons of sugar produced there.

The sugar farmers operate in Washington out of an organization called The Florida Sugar Farmers Association, whose spokesman -- surprise! -- is Bob Buker, the senior vice president of the U.S. Sugar Corporation.

They came to my attention during a review of political TV spending during the primaries where The Sugar Farmers Association turned up consistently, from January through June, as one of the top-10 political time-buyers on the air.

I called Bob Buker, down at U.S. Sugar HQ in Clewiston, Florida, to find out what the hell they were doing with all this TV time.

I called him, in fact, 8 or 9 times over a week's period, and while I waited for Bob to return my call, I dilly-dallied around the net typing "sugar and politics" into the search engines.

Memo to corporate execs who dabble in politics. Always return a reporter's phone calls. You can con 'em, massage 'em, trick 'em or just plain lie to 'em, but never give them time to dilly-dally around the net.

The first thing to pop up was a Florida Online tran-
script of a public radio debate that was to feature Mr.
Buker in a discussion with Mary Barley, chairman of Save
Our Everglades, about the proposed sugar tax amendment.

Although Mr. Buker ducked that one, sending in his
place Alan Rackley, the gist of the issue got laid out
pretty well. Sugar farming in Florida is not an age old
occupation, but really started as a modern day industry in
the early 60's, just after Fidel Castro took over Cuba.

From the late 50's to the late 80's, Florida
acreage under sugar production grew from 35,000 acres to
350,000 acres and today includes 450,000 acres that is
increasingly harvested by machines, thus taking away
that pesky migrant labor issue that in the 70's and 80's
dominated the industry.

In 1988, federal and state environmental authori-
ties filed suit against the sugar growers claiming that
the phosphate run-off from the farms was creating "an
explosion of cattails" and other unnatural foliage in
the Everglades that was drying up the swamp at the rate
of 3-5 acres a day.

Everyone kind of knew it was true. But you can't talk
about killing off the Everglades without acknowledging
that all the Tide poured through all the washing machines
in Miami probably does a certain amount damage to the
swamp, in and of itself, so there are no single villains.

The lawsuit was settled in 1994 through the pas-
sage, in Tallahasee, of The Everglades Forever Act,

which requires sugar farmers to pay $322 million over 20 years, $16 million a year, for pollution control in the Everglades. At the time, the overall clean-up costs were estimated at $750 million to $1 billion. Unfortunately, the latest estimates from the Clinton Administration place the costs closer to $3 billion, and there's a new feeling in Florida that the sugar growers got off light.

A year ago, in November, 1995, when the Republican presidential candidates were jockeying for position at "Presidency III" in Orlando, Sen. Richard Lugar (R-Ind.), chairman of The Senate Agriculture Committee, proposed a 2-cents per pound sugar tax earmarked to fund more clean-up efforts in the Everglades.

Sen. Lugar's sugar tax was part of a 20-year campaign he has waged to end the sugar subsidy entirely in Congress and, when his presidential ambitions went down in flames, he tried to incorporate the tax into the comprehensive Farm Subsidy Revision Act last April.

As *Time* magazine reported (http:www.allpolitics. com), the sugar subsidy survived through a deft maneuver by Senate Majority Leader Bob Dole, who offered opponents an alternative of a $200 million federal Land Reclamation Grant for the Everglades in exchange for leaving the sugar subsidy alone.

Bob ("My word is my bond") Dole obviously was acting only in the public interest and not because Jose F. Fanjul, Sr., one of four brothers who control Flo-Sun, Inc., is a key member of his 1996 presidential campaign finance committee.

Sure, FEC records show Fanjul and other members of his family have given $194,300 to The Republicans since 1991 and he is one of Team 100, the Republican donors committee for people who gave over $100,000. But his brother, Alfonso, was also a 1992 state co-chairman of the Clinton campaign and responsible for $159,728 in contributions to Democrats since 1991.

So it can be said, in all due honesty, the Fanjuls are equal opportunity givers. Since 1991, the FEC records show the family has collectively given $539,528 in contributions to Republicans, Democrats, and other PAC interests.

While waiting for Bob Buker to give me a callback, I had a chance to look up the *Miami Herald's* archival account of the fight on Lexis-Nexis and read Dwight Morris' "Money Talks" account of Florida campaign givers on *PoliticsNow*. I called up the Save Our Everglades web site and learned that Mary Barley is carrying on a crusade her husband, George, a sport fisherman, began a decade ago. He, unfortunately, died in a private airplane crash in 1994 flying back from Tallahasee where he was lobbying for his favorite cause, the Everglades. Their neighbor, Paul Tudor Jones, the head of a Wall Street brokerage firm called Tudor Investments, was personally crushed by the death his friend and agreed to fund the penny-a-pound tax fight to honor George Barley's legacy.

I looked in on the Florida Crystal/Flo-Sun homepage, which explains how the Fanjuls, driven from their 60,000 sugar farm in Cuba by Castro's takeover, bought 4,000 acres in central Florida in 1960 and turned it into a 180,000-acre sugar empire. And I punched "Bob Buker" into the Alta Vista search engine only to discover he is a 41-year-old former helicopter pilot who graduated from the University of Florida law school in 1981, represented "agricultural interests" in a Miami law firm until 1986, joined U.S. Sugar to assist the president in "strategic matters," and oversee the operation of their new citrus processing plant.

One day, just for kicks, I called Bob again at U.S. Sugar. When the secretary asked, "Are you on deadline?" I said, "Yes."

Judy Sanchez, the director of communications for U.S. Sugar, called back inside of ten minutes. "Bob's got a migraine today and is out sick. Can I help you?" she asked.

"Well, you may not believe this," I said. "But you guys are spending more money than God on political advertising this year. What's it all about?"

"Are you familiar with the Save Our Everglades referendum ballot?" she asked.

"A little," I said.

"Well there's a commodity's broker in New York, who trades on the sugar exchange, who provides over 90% of all the money behind this initiative. He has a winter home in Florida, right next door to the head of the Save Our Everglades Committee and, even though he's never given a dime before to environmental causes, he's the man behind it."

"What's his name?" I asked.

"Paul Tudor Jones," she said.

"How much money are you guys willing to throw at this thing?"

"Well, they say they're going to spend $13 million to pass the referendum. We'll spend whatever it takes to keep up," she said.

Now, if you are a political reporter, involved in an issue you know nothing about, you call. . . another political reporter. Mark Washburn, on the state desk of the *Miami Herald*, was particularly helpful.

"This is a very tangled up political issue," he said. "The Everglades are a mess. Is that because sugar farming runoff is ruining them, or because a thousand other interests are encroaching on the territory? **And what are we preserving? The right of alligators to live free? All I know is a lot of people are spending a lot of money on this thing and, in the end, it's all going to wind up in the courts."**

"Why?" I asked.

"Because. . . for instance, what happens if a majority of voters choose amendment 4 (the penny per pound tax), reject amendment 6 (the foundation to control spending of it) and support amendment 2 (requiring a two-thirds majority for constitutional changes)? A judge looked at all of this last month and said, 'Hey, I'm going to embargo the whole thing until after the election -- to see what happens.'"

There was a Mason-Dixon poll in June that showed
60% of the Florida voters supported the "Penny-a-Pound"
tax, 30% opposed it, and 10% were undecided. But that
was before the real TV "issue advertising" appeared.

On September 26th, the last available FEC deadline,
there was enough filing information to show the Save Our
Everglades Committee had raised and spent $4.5 million -
- $4 million donated by Paul Tudor Jones -- to enact the
amendment; and the sugar farming opponents, filing under
the name of the Citizens Committee to Save Jobs and Stop
Unfair Taxes, had raised and spent $6 million (not
including the $2.7 million that the Florida Sugar
Farmers Association spent as an out-of-state committee).

The result has been a series of tit-for-tat political ads on TV in which a pleasure boat fisherman
remembers when the Everglades were pure and wild, and a
harsh voice warns against the loss of jobs created by
"outside interests" in central Florida.

Joe Garcia, the communications director for Save
Our Everglades, told me that since October 1st, his committee has spent, or will spend, about $1 million per
week in the three major TV markets (Miami, Orlando, and
Jacksonville) to bring their message to the voters.
(That's about 1,000 GRP's -- gross rating points -- a
"saturation buy" guaranteeing every TV viewer will see
the commercial at least 3 times.) He believes his opponents, who went on the air two weeks earlier, will match
them GRP for GRP right up to the election.

In the end, if all sides deliver their advertisements as promised, the Florida TV stations will be enriched by about $12 million, which -- if this were Georgia, I'd say -- ain't peanuts.

What I, The Stumpster, like about This Florida Sugar Thing is that an immovable force has met an intractable object. Florida Sugar Money, so used to having it's way in Washington, has run up against a Wall Street investment broker who, liking his fishing, and liking more his former neighbor, said, "Let's not outflank them. Let's outspend them."

Free enterprise! God, isn't that what makes America great?

Why Vote?

Why vote? Well, first off, to pre-serve your right to bitch.

Bitchin' is the American way. Why live here if you can't complain about what's wrong with the place?

The only thing we care about, here in America, is whether you can change it if you don't like it. Can you change the way things are? Anything is possible.

It's easy these days to be a cynic. I am. It's my job. I'm a journalist. I cover the political process and find within it so many absurdities and contradictions it astonishes me that you accept them.

When I write well about the process, you nod along with me and despair of America ever having an honest political discourse. But who the hell cares what you think and why should we?

When I write badly, you pick apart my verbs and modifiers and tell me I use run-on sentences. You take the time to send me letters saying so.

But if you really want to be a professional cynic, if you really want to affect and change society, don't bitch to me. Vote!

When you vote, you separate yourself from the pack by expressing your opinion in a meaningful way. You accept your obligation as a citizen. You stop yakking around the dinner table and apply a little elbow grease to pulling the lever for one candidate or the other. You might, in climates like those I inhabit, have to walk through the rain to get to the polling booth. You might have to stand in line. You might in the vast scheme of things feel inconsequential.

BUT YOU MUST VOTE.

It is proof of your existence.

In Peru, a friend of mine told me, they fine you a month's salary if you do not vote. Your voter registration card is like your driver's license. If it's not marked with your certified fingerprint at the last election, you are not considered a citizen in good standing.

There are plenty of excuses for not voting. You are feeling bad. Your boss has you on deadline. There's no parking around the polling place. You have to be out of town that day.

In Peru, they establish at every polling site a "transient bureau" where out-of-town voters can cast their ballot and not get fined.

In America, we just plain old assume half the eligible voters in the country won't turn out every election because, let's face it, democracy is a broad enough concept to encompass those who participate and those who do not.

So why vote? Why participate at all? Let's say, just for argument sake, we do it out of self-defense.

"People who run for office have to be of marginal intelligence to begin with," Don Rose, a campaign strategist for Martin Luther King, Jane Byrne, and Illinois Governor Jim Edgar once told me. "I mean, who would actually want to run for public office?"

Politicians, Rose would be the first to tell you, gain their esteem from having a majority of people they don't know invest their trust in them.

It's a lonely business. Insurance salesmen do it every day, and suffer the rejections. Lawyers fare better because they only have to pick up the phone, listen some and say, "I think we have a case."

Ministers, or others whom God speaks with directly, will just tell you: God wants you to trust them.

Politicians have a much more complicated task. First, they must make themselves into leaders, then -- as the saying goes -- they must find a parade to get in front of.

As an electorate, our job is to listen and assess and vote for the person, cause, party, or issue that most stimulates our brain. In this election year, our brains have not been stimulated much at all. But political consciousness is important. It is the essence -- the dynamics -- of social governance at work.

If there were no politics, there would be only resentment. The resentment we reserve for a government we have no part in; a government that is, by nature, repressive, and, by definition, provides "taxation without representation."

How quaint to call forward the images of the Boston Tea Party on the eve of this election!

In the compact We The People have written with our country -- long before we, as individual people, had a choice in the matter -- we agreed that government shall be allowed to use taxation to equalize and distribute the benefits of citizenship. This is Rousseau's Social Contract. This is John Locke's Treatise on Liberty. This is the compromise Thomas Jefferson and James Madison hammered out in the Philadelphia halls of the Constitutional Convention. It is the compromise we made to create the right to vote.

The times will never be right for a pure vote. You will never be allowed to walk into a polling booth and "vote your conscience" because. . . that's not what you are supposed to do!

You are supposed to choose. You are supposed to select one guy instead of the other guy -- even though you don't like either of them -- because it matters, in the great data collection system of the country, which one you like more.

If you do not vote, no one will come find and punish you. You will become, quite simply, someone who

222

doesn't matter. Yes, you are a person with opinions. But who the hell cares?

Opinions, not put forth into the public arena, debated and weighed against competing thoughts, judged and voted upon by your fellow citizens, are like unopened fortune cookies. Ideas without vehicles to become reality.

Random thoughts. So pure as to be useless, so uncontaminated by debate as to be considered pristine. An opinion not backed up by a vote is a marble not rolled to the hole. Booty waiting to be collected by the unstoppable demogogues of the playground.

As much as we hate the nature of our political campaigns these days, they are ours. The best minds of our political handlers have found a way to incorporate each of us into a demographic, a winnable or loseable state, a man or woman who might be swayed by this argument or that.

Yes, we might be no more than a cog in the machine. But no one will ever know how that cog really turns until you vote. Your option -- every time you cast a vote -- is to turn against the grain.

Surprise them with your independence. Feel it, think it, do it. Make a decision and maybe, if you are in rhythm with enough of your fellow citizens, you will make a noise.

This year, an estimated 88 million Americans -- about 50% of the voting age population -- will not vote. Dwight Morris and his Campaign Study Group were commissioned by

the Medill School of Journalism to survey the non-partici-
pants and concluded they fall into five "clusters":

* The Doers
* The Unplugged
* The Irritables
* The Don't Knows
* The Alienated

They are a diverse lot with different reasons for
staying away from the polls.

"THE DOERS" (29%) are the largest single group, as a
whole, younger and slightly more educated than the rest.
This year, over 55% earn over $30,000 a year. A member
of this group was more likely to write a letter to an
editor, attend a political rally, and follow political
news last year than the average person who will vote.
But the "Doers" just don't -- for matters of inconve-
nience or disinterest -- turn out to vote.

"THE UNPLUGGEDS" (27%) are also generally younger, less
educated and not given to care about politics. Thirteen
percent said they voted in 1992, 52% said they are going
to vote this year, but 68% aren't even registered.

"THE IRRITABLES" (18%) skew older. They are avid consumers of political news and information, have the
highest incidence of college diplomas (26%), but 65%
agree with the statement "the country has pretty seriously gone off track."

"THE DON'T KNOWS" (14%) are of lower income and lesser
education (25% did not finish high school). They are

more concerned with how to run their own lives than how to run the country.

"THE ALIENATED" (12%) are both the oldest and poorest of the non participants (63% earn less than $30,000 a year). After bitter experience, 52% say they "choose not to vote."

There is a tremendous opportunity to increase electoral participation. Only 100 years ago in 1896, when William Jennings Bryan ran against William McKinley (and only men over the age of 21 could vote), 79% of the eligible voters turned out, including 96% in Illiois. Today in Illinois, that percentage has slipped to less than half the voting population.

Since the voting age was lowered to admit 18-to-20-year-olds into the ranks of citizens in the late Sixties, the percentage of turnout has been on a steady decline.

In 1960, 64% of the voters turned out to choose John Kennedy over Richard Nixon. By 1988, the George Bush-Michael Dukakis race drew an all-time low of 50%. In 1992, voter participation rose to 55%, but among 18-to-20-year-olds, only 12% chose to go to the polls.

People who study the dynamics of voter participation tend to find broad explanations like voter apathy, alienation, or disgust with the candidates. In fact, most people who don't vote have very particular reasons.

A friend of mine teaches a GED class for teenage mothers in a Chicago social service center. She asked her class last week who planned to vote. When only four

of ten admitted they were registered, she asked why.
They didn't want to get put on jury duty, they said.

Yes, with the right to vote comes the responsibility of citizenship. Your vote counts not only on
election day, but is counted on by society all the days
in between.

When you put your name on the roll of eligible voters, you enter the pool of citizens who may be plucked
out at any time to serve on a jury of 12 peers determin-
ing the guilt or innocence of a fellow citizen.

What a great country we have.
By registering to vote, you can actually
vote twice -- once in the polling booth where you may
feel like the needle in the haystack -- and again on a
courtroom jury where your single voice can prevent a
miscarriage of justice. Was citizenship ever more valued, or justified, than in these United States?

**When you cast your ballot, you vote not only for Presidents,
Congressmen, and other officials who will run the government, you
vote to reaffirm your support for a Constitution and court system
that says yes, count me in.** One need only be Black, a woman,
an immigrant, or a Native American (who else is there?) to
imagine a government that doesn't include you.

When you vote, you ultimately elect yourself.

Just by walking into the booth and pulling the
lever, you say I, as a person, have a defensible opinion

about what should happen next and I can be counted on to determine right from wrong. But only if you vote.

Notes and Asides:

You might remember a few opinions back how Half Dead Mitch warned that the plethora of political advertising this month was threatening to derail McDonald's unveiling of the Arch Deluxe campaign.

Sure enough, the October rollout of the Crispy Chicken Arch Deluxe -- "adult food for adults" -- fell flat on its face. The president of the company was exiled to Siberia and all fingers pointed to the poor performance of the media campaign.

I want to make clear that Mitch's dire warnings were in no way responsible for the lackluster rollout, nor was the creative work of the very fine Chicago advertising agency Leo Burnett that now handles the account.

I stopped by McDonald's the other day and, the truth is, the Crispy Chicken Arch Deluxe is one lousy piece of food.

A slab of dried meat sprinkled with shredded lettuce and a dab of mayonnaise on a stale bun? Who are they trying to kid? You don't have to be 73 years old with no tastebuds to be an adult; and if Crispy Chicken Arch Deluxe is what passes for adult food in America today, I'll walk across that bridge to the 21st century arm in arm with the youngest tyke who's willing to hold my hand. Because I think we can do better -- food-wise -- over there than we have over here.

227

If you want to know who Stump is voting for this year, I'm sticking with the Big Mac, goopy but good, which, over on the other side of the bridge, I hear they are already calling The Clinton Burger.

What Does It All Mean?

Well, we did it. We all got together and, after ten months, $2 billion, and innumberable falsehoods, we took a vote to put an end to this whole sordid affair we're calling Campaign '96.

For the record, Bill Clinton will continue for a second term in the White House because 45,628,667 people voted for him, 37,869,435 voted for Bob Dole, and 7,874,283 voted for Ross Perot.

Officially -- if you go by the Electoral College -- Clinton has won the control of 379 delegates, Dole has 159, and Perot has none.

What does it all mean?

If you follow Stump's argument that we all pretty much go into the booth and vote for ourselves, it may mean no more than this:

Bill Clinton was 23 years closer and more in tune with the concerns of the average American at the end of this century -- who is, by the way, a 32.7-year-old white woman -- than the other guys.

You can read the exit polls any way you want. The voters like a good economy; they want the push and tug of a Republican Congress and Democratic White House; they think character is *an* issue but not *the* issue in choosing a president.

What will soon dawn on the country is that America didn't decide on a president last Tuesday, we decided on a Special Prosecutor who, if he does his job right, will spend the next four years sending The President and A Majority of Congress to jail for campaign law violations.

The brouhaha over President Clinton's fundraising among Asian-Americans gave the final days of the campaign a welcome jolt of reality about what the campaign is really about. Where have you reporters, you alleged boys on the bus, been these last five months?

John Huang's arm-twisting of Korean, Indonesian, and Taiwanese businessmen was so blatant that even a punch drunk Bob Dole, cruising around on his 96 Hours to Retirement Party, could score points with it. Ross Perot doubled his pre-election poll numbers just by holding the flame of ridicule up to Clinton's fundraising.

The net-net of all this is that The Justice Department -- which already has independent counsels investigating Hillary on Whitewater, Mike Espy in the Agriculture

Department, Henry Cisneros in HUD, and Ron Brown's appoint-
ments in Commerce -- will have to name another to look into
this year's campaign law infractions by Congress, the White
House, the Democratic, and the Republican Parties.

I call them "campaign infractions," but of course
they are really, out and out, bald-faced money grabs.

The $425,000 contribution from an Indonesian couple
associated with the Lippo Group; the $250,000 gift the
Democrats had to return to a South Korean businessman; the
$140,000 raised in a Buddhist temple in Los Angeles cour-
tesy of an appearance by Al Gore; and the $325,000 donated
to the Democratic National Committee by a distant relative
of Mahatma Gandhi are only the tip of the iceberg.

If that's what the foreigners were giving to get access to the White House, what
were the President's operatives promising the
Americans who donated the other $399 million?

And what did the candidates for the House and Senate
have to promise to get together the $800 million
bankrolls they raised to pursue public office?

At last count, there were nine Congressional investigating committees preparing inquiries into federal
campaign law violations. Targets were squirting out of
the news pages of every major daily last week:

>James C.Wood, the U.S. liason to the Taiwan
Institute in Taipai, who hosted fundraising events for
Chinese businessmen even though foreigners are barred
from contributing to American campaigns.

>Mark E. Middleton, another campaign fundraiser who reportedly solicited a $15 million contribution from a Taiwan political party using a White House business card that had direct dial phone numbers for himself and Mack McLarty, Clinton's former chief of staff.

>Webster Hubbell, Hillary's senior partner in the Rose Law Firm, who joined the Justice Department, stepped down in controversy, and then represented, surprise, the Lippo Group.

With the press yapping at his heels, Clinton was forced to declare himself in favor of campaign finance reform (even though he has been the chief beneficiary of the current system) in the lamest kind of *mea culpa*.

"Everybody knows the problems of campaign money today," Clinton told a rally in Santa Barbara, California, on November 1st, the Friday before the election. "There's too much of it. It takes too much time to raise and it raises too many questions."

"We have played by the rules. But I know, and you know, we need to change the rules," Clinton said.

On *Washington Week in Review*, David Broder, the dean of political columnists for the *Washington Post*, and Ken Bode, an NBC correspondent and program host, commented the following Sunday (two days before the election):

"The rules have been shredded to such a point it's practically a wide open game," Broder said. Bode played an audiotape recording of Middleton's White House answering machine message.

"If this is playing by the rules," there really are no rules," Bode said.

As I write this, the TV networks are escalating their estimates on the influence of money on politics. Dan Rather now claims that on election eve, political campaign spending this year -- on the federal level alone -- will exceed $2 billion.

The ABC-affiliated website *PoliticsNow* has a story reporting the candidates have been pouring $5 million a day into TV advertising for most of last month.

What's wrong with this picture? It's a system out of control. As Clinton says: You know it, I know it, he knows it, the Republicans know it, the Democrats know it, the incumbents know it, the challengers know it. And nobody has done anything about it.

That's why a Special Prosecutor to investigate campaign finance violations is kind of a neat idea. As vague as the law may be, as soft as soft money sounds, the hard reality is **we are dealing with MONEY pumped into the political system by people who want specific "strategic" advantages as a result of their contributions.**

They are so intent on gaining that advantage they look for ways to give more than the $1,000 limit Congress placed on contributions to candidate, much more.

Were you a good citizen? Did you vote? Did you work your precinct? Did you give your best friend $100 at a

coffee klatsch so she could run for the state legisla-
ture? That's how politics was meant to work.

But that's not how it worked this year. The *New York
Times* had an article on Sunday, November 3rd, under the
headline "For Asian-Americans, Political Power Can Lead
to Harsh Scrutiny."

Two key paragraphs stood out. Here they are:

*"We'd been sending the softest of soft money before
because it wasn't bundled and we were afraid to ask for
anything in return," said Thomas Chan, a Los Angeles
lawyer and chairman of Chinese Americans Unite for Self
Empowerment, or CAUSE. "There were no strings attached
and so nobody would listen to us, which is what you're
seeing today. Now, many of us want to make the contributions work better."*

*David Lang, a professional fundraiser in Los Angeles
who works mostly with Asian Americans, said the effort to
use political donations more effectively began after the
1992 election, when he talked with Jewish groups about
their fundraising methods and then discussed the ideas with
other Asian Americans. The result was to bundle more donations to build a series of political action committees.
"Nothing happens unless we're organized," Mr. Lang said.*

"Organized giving" is the downfall of campaign financing.

It started with the formation of special-interest
money into "political action committees." But when you
bring people together with the specific goal of influ-
encing the political process, inevitably one of them

says, "What if I spend more? How much more influence can I have?"

If you are wise to the loopholes in The Campaign Reform Act of 1974, you say, "How much do you want to spend -- $10,000, $50,000, $500,000? Tell me the level on which you want to give, and I'll show you a way to make it legal."

The disgrace of this campaign is that people went and wrote the check. And the politicians cashed it -- without a second thought.

Already, B. J. Thornberry, who oversees campaign finances for the Democratic National Committee, has admitted her staff was so "awash in cash," they abandoned an internal system of background checks on large donors because they couldn't keep up with the paperwork.

In Washington, they will gently debate whether campaign contributions provided "access" to high office that ordinary citizens could not achieve. Were the contributions properly recorded? Were "shell" con- tributors used? Was "soft" money transferred into "hard" partisan spending?

In Chicago, we have a political expression we'd like to contribute to the national debate: Bribery.

What if The Special Prosecutor skips all this "fail- ure to disclose" malfeasance and goes out in search of the "quid pro quo" that makes a bribe a bribe?

We have had a little experience with bribery here in Illinois. We know there are two statutory levels for indictment: The "strict" bribe in which money is given and the parking ticket is fixed; and "soft bribery" where money is given "with the expectation of favorable treatment" and received "with the knowledge a favor is requested."

The "quid pro quo" -- literally, "this for that" -- would be an act or vote by the President or member of Congress that resulted in favorable treatment for a campaign contributor.

This would create a new paradigm in Washington. If you received a contribution of $1,000 or more from a party with legislation before Congress, your vote on any aspect of the legislation -- from a subcommittee mark-up session to a motion for closure of a filibuster -- would become "sufficient cause" for a special prosecutor to issue subpoenas and order wiretaps on all conversations you have had, or are now having, with lobbyists associated with any future issue you may vote upon.

If that becomes the criterion for a Congressman expressing an honest, publicly-supported opinion of his constituents, it might revolutionize politics. You might say, no politician would pass that test of innocence. That is all too true.

But in our court system, people do not have to prove their innocence. The prosecutor must prove their guilt. The burden remains on the Special Prosecutor to uncover the underlying promises and conversations

236

behind the campaign gifts, and show how the expectation was made explicit.

If a Special Prosecutor approaches this year's campaign financing not as a violation of Federal Election Commission rules but as 10,000 potentially criminal acts based on the bribery statutes, it would really turn Washington on its ear.

Reform in Chicago politics did not come about until the U.S. Attorney's office took the RICO laws enacted in the 70's to stop organized crime and turned them against the politicians with wiretaps, undercover agents, and sophisticated financial tracking of bank accounts and tax returns tht proved gangsterism and politics were not so far apart.

In the 90's, a similiar wave of reform will come about only when a Special Prosecutor uses today's best legal weapon -- the computer -- to pursue these same crimes.

We live in a world of databases. There is a database inside the FEC of political contributors who gave over $1,000. There is also, thanks to Newt Gingrich, a database of Congressional votes on every committee vote, amendment and final floor vote that every House and Senate member has ever cast on any piece of legislation that passes through our Congress.

Let's run the data. And not just for Bill Clinton, but all the others and, especially, anybody who has, or will have, a seat in Congress next year.

Let's work our way through the special interests one industry at a time -- sugar, tobacco, entertainment, broadcasting, health care, telecommunications, banking, Wall Street, automotive -- with the understanding a political contribution of over $1,000 that results in a favorable vote on legislation affecting the contributor is the essential "quid pro quo" needed to undertake a bribery investigation, indictment, and conviction.

Under these rules, Washington over the next two years would be a mighty different place. When the tobacco subsidy program comes up for review, Congressmen would face three options -- voting for, voting against, or "recusing" themselves on an issue in which they have a potential conflict of interest.

Imagine what the tobacco lobbyists, who threw all that money at incumbents, will say when "their Congressman" turns around and abstains because their contributions were given "with the expectation" he would vote their way.

A Special Prosecutor who takes his post seriously will see his office as a mandate to look at the whole range of campaign contributions this last year.

Clinton's violations are easy meat. If they don't get him on Whitewater or Paula Jones, they'll nail him for FEC disclosure violations. But, by then, it will be the year 2000 and no one will care.

Let the Special Prosecutor on Campaign Infractions not be distracted. Let him pursue his investigation with an eye toward patterns of corruption, and dispatch his investigators to amass the kind of multi-count indictment that sent Danny Rostenkowski to jail for sending out too many free ashtrays from the Congressional store.

If the Special Prosecutor does his job, Bill Clinton won't be the only guy going to jail. The whole kit and kaboodle are going to go down.

I say we start the prosecutions now, lock 'em all up and throw away the key. And when we cross that bridge to the 21st century, we dynamite it behind us.

It was Stump's intention after the election to take a four-year hiatus back in the cabin on the foothills of Iron Mountain. But if this Special Prosecutor thing gets going, I may have to move to Washington.

This could be the most fun we've had since Watergate.

//stump.stuff
@ index

Acknowledgments

Over the course of the political campaign, many people contributed to the shape and writing of these columns. Those who contributed most were my friends and colleagues around IPA, that very fine post house on Webster Street, and especially, Gina Bardi, David Blum, Bob Brink, Deb Cottle, Jan Collins, Casey Stockdon, Melissa Taylor, Marilyn Wulff, and David Zerlin.

I want to also thank Bruce and Lorelei Bendinger of The Copy Workshop, designer R Jamie Apel, and copy editor Melissa Davis (Kevin, too). Special thanks to Tom Weinberg and Lucy Domino for their friendship and encouragement.

STUMP. A Campaign Journal

designed by R Jamie Apel
and set in 11pt letter gothic
[for the most part] with
a little rotis sans , FRANKLIN
GOTHIC, OCRA┐ & american typewriter
pretty much thrown in just
for the hell of it.